THE TEACHING OF
DRAWING

ITS AIMS AND METHODS

BY

S. POLAK

ART MASTER : INSTRUCTOR IN DRAWING UNDER THE LONDON COUNTY COUNCIL
AUTHOR OF "THE THEORY AND PRACTICE OF PERSPECTIVE DRAWING"

AND

H. C. QUILTER

INSTRUCTOR IN DRAWING UNDER THE MIDDLESEX COUNTY COUNCIL

British Library Cataloguing-in-Publication Data
A catalogue record for this book is available from the
British Library

Drawing and Illustration

Drawing is a form of visual art that can make use of any number of drawing instruments, including graphite pencils, pen and ink, inked brushes, wax colour pencils, crayons, charcoal, chalk, pastels and various kinds of erasers, markers, styluses, metals (such as silverpoint) and even electronic drawing. As a medium, it has been one of the most popular and fundamental means of public expression throughout human history – as one of the simplest and most efficient means of communicating visual ideas.

Drawing itself long predates other forms of human communication, with evidence for its existence preceding that of the written word – demonstrated in cave paintings of around 40,000 years ago. These drawings, known as pictograms, depicted objects and abstract concepts including animals, human hands and generalised patterns. Over time, these sketches and paintings were stylised and simplified, leading to the development of the written language as we know it today. This form of drawing can truly be considered art in its purest sense – the basic forms on which all others build.

Whilst the term 'to draw' derives from the Old English *dragan* (meaning 'to drag, draw or protract'), the word 'illustrate' derives from the Latin word *illustratio*, meaning 'enlighten' or 'irradiate'. This process of 'enlightenment' is central to drawing and illustration as we know it today. Medieval codices' illustrations were often called 'illuminations', designed to highlight and further explain important aspects of biblical texts. This was the most general form of illustration; hand-created, individual and unique. This changed in the fifteenth century however, when books began to be illustrated with woodcuts – most notably in Germany, by Albrecht Dürer.

The first creative impulses of a painter or sculptor are commonly expressed in drawings, and architects and photographers are commonly trained to draw, if for no other reason than to train their perceptual skills and develop their creative potential. Initially, artists used and re-used wooden tablets for the production of their drawings, however following the widespread availability of paper in the fourteenth century, the use of drawing in the arts increased. During the Renaissance (a period of massive flourishing of human intellectual endeavours and creativity), drawings exhibiting realistic and representational qualities emerged. Notable draftsmen included Leonardo da Vinci, Michelangelo and Raphael. They were inspired by the concurrent developments in geometry and philosophy, exhibiting a true synthesis of these branches – a combination somewhat lost in the modern day.

Figure drawing became a recognised subsection of artistic drawing in this period, despite its long history stretching back to prehistoric descriptions. An anecdote by the Roman author and philosopher Pliny, describes how Zeuxis (a painter who flourished during the 5th century BCE) reviewed the young women of Agrigentum naked before selecting five whose features he would combine in order to paint an ideal image. The use of nude models in the medieval artist's workshop is further implied in the writings of Cennino Cennini (an Italian painter), and a manuscript of Villard de Honnecourt confirms that sketching from life was an established practice by the thirteenth century. The Carracci, who opened their *Accademia degli Incamminati* (one of the first art academies in Italy) in Bologna in the 1580s, set the pattern for later art schools by making life drawing the central discipline. The course of training began with the copying of engravings, then proceeded to drawing from plaster casts, after which the students were trained in drawing from the live model.

The main processes for reproduction of drawings and illustrations in the sixteenth and seventeenth centuries were engraving and etching, and by the end of the eighteenth century, lithography (a method of printing originally based on the immiscibility of oil and water) allowed even better illustrations to be reproduced. In the later seventeenth and eighteenth centuries, the previous combination of the arts and sciences in drawing gave way to a more romantic and even classical style, epitomised by draftsmen such as Poussin, Rembrandt, Rubens, Tiepolo and Antoine Watteau. Mastery in drawing was considered a prerequisite to painting, and students in Jacques-Louis David's Studio (a famed eighteenth century French painter of the neo-classical style), were required to draw for six hours a day, from a model who remained in the same pose for an entire week!

During this period, an increasingly large gap started to emerge between 'fine artists' on the one hand, and 'draftsmen' / 'illustrators' on the other. This difference became further complicated with the 'Golden Age of Illustration'; a period customarily defined as lasting from the latter quarter of the nineteenth century until just after the First World War. In this period of no more than fifty years the popularity, abundance and most importantly the unprecedented upsurge in quality of illustrated works marked an astounding change in the way that publishers, artists and the general public came to view artistic drawing. Arthur Rackham, Walter Crane, John Tenniel and William Blake are some of its most famous names. Until the latter part of the nineteenth century, the work of illustrators was largely proffered anonymously, and in England it was only after Thomas Bewick's pioneering technical advances in wood engraving that it became common to acknowledge the artistic and technical expertise of illustrators. Such draftsmen also frequently used their drawings in preparation for paintings, further obfuscating the distinction between drawing/painting, high/low art.

The artists involved in the Arts and Crafts Movement (with a strong emphasis on stylised drawing, and a powerful influence on the 'Golden Age of Illustration') also attempted to counter the ever intruding Industrial Revolution, by bringing the values of beautiful and inventive craftsmanship back into the sphere of everyday life. This helped to counter the main challenge which emerged around this time – photography. The invention of the first widely available form of photography (with flexible photographic film role marketed in 1885) led to a shift in the use of drawing in the arts. This new technology took over from drawing as a superior method of accurately representing the visual world, and many artists abandoned their painstaking drawing practices. As a result of these developments however, modernism in the arts emerged – encouraging 'imaginative originality' in drawing and abstract formulations. Drawing was once again at the forefront of the arts.

There are many different categories of drawing, including figure drawing, cartooning, doodling and shading. There are also many drawing methods, such as line drawing, stippling, shading, hatching, crosshatching, creating textures and tracing – and the artist must be aware of complex problems such as form, proportion and perspective (portrayed in either linear methods, or depth through tone and texture). Today, there are also many computer-aided drawing tools, which are utilised in design, architecture, engineering, as well as the fine arts. It is often exploratory, with considerable emphasis on observation, problem-solving and composition, and as such, remains an unceasingly useful tool in the artists repertoire.

The processes of drawing is a fascinating artistic practice, enabling a beautiful array of effects and creative expression. As is evident from this short introduction, it also has an incredibly old history, moving from decorations on cave walls to the most advanced, realistic and imaginative drawings possible in the present day. It is hoped that the current reader enjoys this book on the subject.

PREFACE.

At the present time our methods of education are undergoing considerable change ; the old conventional ideas are receiving new and wider meanings.

In no subject is this change more apparent than in the teaching of Drawing. The old freehand copy and geometrical model are fast disappearing and our pupils are set to study *real* things. In other words, once more in the history of Art the "Classical" is giving way to the "natural," and we are endeavouring to leave tradition in order to bring our methods into line with present ideals.

But in all changes it is prudent to proceed cautiously, and in this book an attempt is made to preserve what is good in old methods while pointing out the best ways of commencing and pursuing newer and more educational courses.

In the arrangement of the present work the subjects, where possible, have been set out in suitable *Stages* marking the order of study. Except in the case of Conventional Ornament, which is unsuitable below the third standard, these Stages are intended to correspond with the Standards in an elementary school. It is impossible, however, to lay down a fixed rule as to the rate of progress : this must be determined largely by special circumstances. Thus, where

a subject such as Brushwork and Colour Study is introduced at a late period of school life more than one Stage
may be taken in each Standard.

The value of Drawing as a means of education is
receiving greater recognition than formerly in all educational circles, and especially by the Board of Education.
It is hoped that teachers, who now have a free hand in
formulating their schemes of drawing instruction, will
find useful guidance in these pages as to the respective
merits of the various branches of elementary drawing,
and that the methods that have been successfully employed
by the authors will be found of practical value by others.

S. POLAK,
H. C. QUILTER.

CONTENTS.

CHAPTER I.

THE VALUE OF DRAWING.—GENERAL PRINCIPLES OF TEACHING.

*Learn drawing—that you may set down clearly, and usefully, records of such things as cannot be described in words, either to assist your own memory of them, or to convey distinct ideas of them to other people; to obtain quicker perceptions of the beauty of the natural world and to preserve something like a true image of beautiful things that pass away . . . to understand the minds of great painters and to appreciate their work sincerely.—*RUSKIN.

1. The Place of Drawing in Education.—Drawing is not only a subject of great aesthetic and practical value, but an important means of mental development and a useful adjunct to the teaching of other subjects of the school curriculum.

A perfect adjustment to our surroundings is the aim of education and a great part of our knowledge of our environment is derived through the senses of sight and touch with which Drawing is mainly connected,

Drawing is a *natural* means of education. The delight which the youngest children take in representing familiar forms, and the interest in the subject which may be aroused so easily are proofs of this. Under proper guidance this instinct may be developed in such a way as to be a life-long source of enjoyment and a means of self-improvement.

As regards its practical value, Drawing may be called "the shorthand of expression." A few strokes of the pencil will often convey an idea far more adequately than the longest verbal description. The ability to reproduce form and colour is often indispensable in the occupation chosen by the child later in life.

2. Cultivation of the Power of Drawing.—It has been rightly asserted that the power to draw moderately well can be attained by all. The class-teacher, at least, must work on this assumption. Where the child's powers of eye, mind, and hand are so happily adjusted as to result in a natural aptitude for drawing, the teacher's task is light and much of his teaching superfluous. Unfortunately such instances are exceptional. An observant or intelligent child may be lacking in muscular control, a dexterous child may exhibit weakness in the power of observation, while others (and these constitute a fair proportion of the whole) may be deficient in all the essential gifts.

General practice is usually relied on for the cultivation of the power of drawing, but the practical teacher, at some time or other, will be impelled to devise exercises for strengthening particular functions of the hand and eye. Within certain limits, technical exercises are as useful in Drawing as in any other art.

Care must, however, be taken to make these exercises interesting and not so protracted as to create a distaste for the subject or destroy spontaneous effort. We should not insist on extreme precision in drawing in young children.

The exercises advocated here, such as Imaginary Drawing, for the purpose of sharpening the observation, or for manipulative training, may be practised for a few minutes at the beginning of the lesson and gradually discontinued as progress is made. In order that the utmost value may be extracted from them special attention should be given to the backward children, and great care must be taken to see that the exercises are not performed in a perfunctory manner.

3. The Natural Order of Practice.—Control of the muscles of the shoulder and arm is obtained sooner than that of the wrist and fingers. This naturally suggests the order of practice and the exclusive use of free-arm movements at first. The lack of power in infants suggests the use of a medium that will offer the least resistance to free movement. Hence the value, for babies, of drawing in sand. When the child is able to grip better, a soft yielding instrument, such as charcoal, chalk, or crayon, should be employed.

The *brush*, although offering great difficulties as regards complete control, being a light, flexible instrument, responding to the slightest impulse of the will, may be used next.

When the child has obtained sufficient control over the muscles of the wrist and fingers the lead pencil should be employed. In the meantime he will probably have had some practice in writing, which is a form of drawing.

This book does not treat of the many allied occupations, such as paper-folding and clay-modelling, but their value in the way of hand and eye training and as a means of acquiring first-hand knowledge cannot be over-estimated.

4. Aims of the Teacher.—The teacher should endeavour to create and foster a love of drawing, especially' where little liking or aptitude for the subject is shown. For this purpose he must understand the working of the child's mind, excite and retain his interest by introducing variety in the work, showing him its utility, and in other ways. The following paragraphs show how these aims may be realised.

5. Variety of Work.—*Colour* has great attraction for children, and should therefore be employed largely in the early stages. The exercises should deal with actual and interesting objects, such as a simple flower, fruit, or familiar toy. As the child gets older the examples may become more formal, but the total substitution of abstract for concrete forms should never take place. Children find far greater interest in drawing from things than from representations of them.

Teachers frequently complain of the crowding of the Drawing Syllabus, especially when entirely new methods of expression are introduced, such as colour, light, and shade.

Although new methods take time to acquire, it must be remembered that variety is a very important factor in the teaching of elementary drawing. This is proved by the eagernesss with which children take to a new mode of expression and the increased earnestness of their work when perhaps they would have lost interest in drawing in a single style. It is neither necessary nor advisable to wait until anything like perfection in drawing in one medium is reached before proceeding to a second. The main principles of drawing are common to all forms of expression, and practice in one method must promote proficiency in another.

6. Correlation.—The correlation of Drawing with other subjects of instruction should be constant. No scheme of general education can be considered complete that does not take the possibilities of Drawing into account. Besides its necessity, the child is interested and loves to see the applicability of his studies.

The correlation may be in connection with (1) other branches of hand and eye training, e.g. clay modelling, paper folding, woodwork, metalwork, etc.; (2) general subjects of instruction, e.g. writing, arithmetic and mensuration, composition, geography, history, science, or observation lessons.

Correlation of work is an important feature in Kindergarten training, one subject frequently forming the theme of the various lessons of the week. Much time is of course devoted to varied occupations; yet the usual sudden break from the pleasant, varied work of the lower school to the more solid study of the upper is to be regretted. This gap may be bridged in a measure by continuing such subjects as chalk and brush drawing, and especially direct nature drawing.

7. Imaginative and Inventive Drawing.—Very little of the higher and creative forms of art can be attained in the elementary school. The teacher is chiefly concerned with laying the foundations of accurate observation and interpretation. Nevertheless, much may be done to encourage and develop the child's imagination and invention. His ability to create and adapt will grow with his powers of expression and knowledge of form.

The power of expression is rarely able to keep pace with that of the imagination. The child's apparently meaningless scribble, however, may have a great deal of meaning for him, just as the young infant's prattle may be an effort to give expression to thought. If, therefore, Imaginative Drawing cannot be taken as a subject of serious study, it is highly important that we should take into account any aesthetic taste, power of imagination, or invention from the very beginning, and afford our pupils opportunities and encouragement for spontaneous effort.

8. Cultivation of the Aesthetic Sense.—The appreciation of beauty of form and colour, though difficult to inculcate, should form an important part of the child's education. The development of the aesthetic sense is largely dependent on environment. Unfortunately, this is often most unfavourable in the case of children attending Public Elementary Schools.

The choice of objects for drawing should be influenced as far as possible by beauty of form and colour. Important principles of beauty are explained in the body of this work, especially in the chapters on Colour and Nature Drawing. The training, however, must be continual, and much of it unconscious on the part of the pupil.

Thus, an attempt should be made to rise above mere orderliness of the class-room by the introduction of simple decorative objects, such as flowers and plants, pictures and photographs. These need not be many or expensive. The commonest objects are often the most beautiful. A handful of cut flowers will provide a lesson on tasteful arrangement in which the children's assistance and opinion may be invited. Even the child's personal appearance may come in, occasionally, for a few words of criticism on the part of the teacher.

The country child is brought nearer the beauties existing in nature than the town child, yet these silent influences, from their very familiarity, often leave his mind unaffected. The feeling for beauty sometimes needs stimulus and regular guidance.

A town child, on the other hand, may show great appreciation of the limited opportunities afforded by the humble garden, the park, or an occasional glimpse of the country. He has far greater facilities, however, for studying the beautiful works of man, in the museums, picture galleries and buildings of architectural importance. Unfortunately, as in the case of the country child, valuable opportunities are neglected. It is to be deplored that for the want of a little early education the wealth of architectural beauty existing in many of our large towns appeals in vain to the senses of the majority of the passersby. An elementary treatise on architecture will put the teacher in possession of the main points that distinguish the various styles of architecture, and concrete examples may be found in local public buildings.

9. Conduct of the Drawing Lesson.—No subject requires so much thought in drawing up a suitable scheme of instruction and in the logical arrangement of exercises. These should be carefully graduated so that few difficulties, those actually intended, are presented at a time. Otherwise difficulties frequently crop up in the course of a lesson which, if anticipated, might have led to the exercise being postponed or rejected.

As to the method in which the lesson should be conducted the practical teacher will not go far wrong if he be guided by the principles that should govern good teaching generally. Great differences of opinion, however, prevail at the present day in the matter of Drawing, and the extremes may be described as

(1) The " **All-Guidance** " **Method,** and

(2) The " **No-Guidance** " **Method.**

10. The "All-Guidance" Method of Teaching.— In this it is laid down that the teacher should act the part of the *scout*: call the children's attention to all the "points," such as proportions and peculiarities of structure, warn them of the pitfalls and difficulties and show them how they should be met. While the teacher is *talking*, the children, who probably are eager to *draw*, lose all interest in the lesson as well as much of their time. The exercise will be worked then, perhaps, step by step from the blackboard.

This method may result in a neat and uniform style of drawing and afford a certain amount of technical practice, but it must be condemned as being uneducational. The teacher may have worked very hard, but the children have missed the opportunity of exercising observation, judgment, and self-reliance.

11. The "No-Guidance" Method of Teaching.— The copy or object is placed before the children with the simple injunction, "Draw what you see." This method must be condemned also. It may be adopted occasionally as a form of test, but if continued time after time the child must meet with difficulties with which he cannot cope. He wanders in a veritable *cul-de-sac* of study, never expressing more than partial truths, and at last loses interest in the work. The teacher in the meantime finds so much to criticise and to correct that he, too, gives it up in despair.

12. A Rational Method of Teaching.— We shall find it best to steer a middle course between these extremes. If explanation seems necessary, it should be restricted. The exercise must be carefully chosen so as to be within the capacity of the average pupil. We should impose as little convention as possible, encourage individuality by compelling the child to exercise his judgment to the utmost of his powers. When this course fails, the nature of individual errors and the method of rectifying them may be elicited by skilful questioning, and then, if necessary, we should not hesitate to give positive instruction.

13. Relation between Teacher and Scholars.—The teacher may often find much to condemn in a child's drawing, but he should also be on the look-out for what is praiseworthy. The attempt may be crude, yet if it show honest effort or some improvement, the teacher should acknowledge the fact, *before* calling attention to defects. Nothing is more apt to dishearten a child than to find that his earnest endeavours are not recognised. On the other hand, a word of sympathy or commendation may live in a child's memory and become an incentive to persevere throughout life.

14. Criticism and Correction of Work.—Every drawing should be seen and criticised at or before the end of the lesson. Should the child get the notion that his good drawing may pass unnoticed or his bad drawing escape censure, the quality of his work may deteriorate rather than improve. Much of the value of criticism is lost if delayed to a subsequent lesson.

Where the class is large and the lesson short, this matter of individual criticism is a difficult one, but the time should be allotted. If a system of marking be adopted it may be simplified; thus, a " tick " may denote satisfactory, and a " cross " unsatisfactory work.

Concerning the **correction of drawings,** the child's feelings should be considered. His sensitive nature rebels against the scoring of his cherished work with the blue pencil. On the other hand, it is equally bad policy to make a great many corrections in the medium employed by the scholar, so that in the end less of his work is apparent than the teacher's. This may be better for the appearance of the copy, but not for the child's morals. He is likely to cheat himself into the belief that the result is due to his own efforts, when perhaps the only good parts of the drawing are those done by the teacher. Further, the knowledge that his work will be improved for him may incline him to carelessness.

The following method is suggested :—The teacher should move quickly round the class while the work is in progress, paying extra attention to the weak draughtsmen.

Attention should be called to faults, but the exact nature of these should not be stated by the teacher. The child should be led to recognise them, by means of questioning if necessary, and to suggest the remedy himself.

Where the error is due to lack of power of expression or is of a technical nature, such as the handling of the pencil or brush, *the teacher should pattern the drawing at the side of the child's,* leaving him to improve his own attempt. If the error be a common one, it must be made the subject of class demonstration and the same difficulty introduced in the next lesson. In this way evidence of the teacher's supervision will be given in the gradual improvement of the children's work rather than by an elaborate system of marking and correction of exercises.

CHAPTER II.

VARIOUS MEDIA AND MODES OF EXPRESSION.

It is desirable, and indeed is necessary to intellectual health that the mind should be recreated and refreshed with a variety in our studies; that in the irksomeness of uniform pursuit we should be relieved, and, if I may say so, deceived as much as possible. Besides the minds of men are so very differently constituted, that it is impossible to find one method that shall be suitable to all.—SIR JOSHUA REYNOLDS.

15. Classification of Subjects of Instruction.—The various branches of instruction in Drawing, apart from mechanical drawing, suitable in elementary schools admit of various methods of classification; thus :—

(1) **According to the Instrument Employed**—

    (*a*) Drawing with the **Firm Point,** such as the finger in sand, chalk and crayon on the blackboard, millboard and paper of various kinds, slate and pencil, lead pencil, and pen.

    (*b*) Drawing with the **Flexible Point**—the brush.

(2) **According to the Mode of Execution;** thus :—
    (*a*) Freearm, (*b*) Freehand, (*c*) Brush Drawing.

(3) **According to the Subject of Study;** thus :—
    (*a*) Conventional Ornament, (*b*) Model and Object Drawing, (*c*) Nature Drawing, (*d*) Design, (*e*) Memory Drawing, (*f*) Imaginative Drawing.

16. Drawing in Sand.—This is a useful exercise for the babies in the Infant School. Each child is provided with a shallow tray of silver sand. The children become highly interested in marking various forms with the finger or with a pointed stick. By shaking the tray the level surface of the sand can be renewed. They may be asked to draw letters of the alphabet, common objects, or illustrate fairy stories. They like to draw the postman, the blacksmith, father, mother, and so on. Of course their efforts often appear ludicrous, but a sympathetic teacher will be able to see an element of truth in most cases. The chief value of the exercise lies in the employment of the hand and eyes.

FREEARM DRAWING.

17. Definition.—As the name implies, Freearm is that method of drawing in which the arm is moved independently of any supporting surface. Differences of opinion exist as to what constitute the proper movements. By some the term is applied to any form of drawing on a more or less vertical surface in which the movements may be performed by the forearm, wrist and fingers independently of the upper arm and in any medium such as chalk, crayon, pencil, and even brush. Drawing with the arm fully extended, the movement coming from the shoulder, is then sometimes distinguished as *Shoulder Work*. Others maintain that the latter is the only true form of Freearm Drawing.

18. Its Value.—Whatever is strictly implied by the term, no doubt can exist as to the value of this form of drawing, especially for young children. Its value is in proportion to the extent the arm is stretched and the consequent size of the drawing. Large drawings are a *sine quâ non* for young children.

The position of the body, whether standing or sitting, and the distance of the eye from the drawing surface make Freearm the most hygienic method of drawing.

Much of the child's early training is concerned with the mastery of the pencil or pen as a *writing* instrument. As the movements of the hand in writing differ somewhat ·from those in drawing, practice in both methods concurrently when neither has been mastered must be disadvantageous. By the nature of the movements, Freearm Drawing has the further merit that it leads to a swift, vigorous, and easy style, and if continued later, alternately with other methods, acts as a good corrective for the painful, niggling style of drawing that sometimes prevails.

19. Disadvantages.—On the other hand, exclusive practice in Freearm Drawing among older scholars cannot be recommended. It becomes necessary, ultimately, to draw on a more limited surface and in a more permanent medium than chalk, crayon, charcoal, etc., and the quality of the work may suffer for the delay in the training of the muscles of the fingers and wrist.

If we compare the drawing of a child who has been trained on Freearm methods with that of a child of equal capacity whose practice has been restricted to *Freehand*, the former will be distinguished probably by better proportion and general notion of form, but might be loose and careless in detail and lack the precision of the latter style. We must conclude, therefore, that it is best to take Freearm Drawing exclusively till about the sixth year, and concurrently with Freehand and in gradually lessening amount in later years.

VARIOUS METHODS OF CONDUCTING FREEARM
DRAWING LESSONS.

20. Drawing in a Standing Position.—Drawing with chalk on the blackboard is the best but least available method. Teacher and children work in the same way. The drawing surface offers a good " bite " and its tone a strong contrast to the chalk. The use of white on black for drawing and demonstration purposes is condemned by some medical authorities, but the exercise is rarely protracted enough to have any evil effects on the sight.

The boards may be of the continuous type affixed to the walls of the class-room or school hall, each scholar's space being clearly marked off ; or separate small boards may be placed in a slightly sloping position on narrow ledges fitted round the walls. The height of these ledges and the size of the boards should vary according to the size of the scholars. The boards may be from about 15″ × 20″ in the lowest to 24″ × 36″ in the highest classes.

A space of a few feet is necessary in order that the children may stand well back while at work and view their work occasionally from a distance. The school hall is therefore best suited for the purpose. If the lesson be conducted in the class-room it may be necessary to move the desks further from the walls. Should the accommodation be insufficient for the whole class, one section may be employed at a time, the remainder working the exercise at their desks.

Linoleum, millboards, or coarse paper attached to the latter with metal clips may be used in the same way as these small blackboards.

21. Method of Work.—Each child is provided with white or coloured chalk and duster for blackboard work. The first exercises should consist of swinging circular movements, the arm being fully stretched and describing a cone of which the shoulder is the apex.

The body is held erect, in an easy position, and square to the board. The arm should be swung towards the left and right alternately, the movements being fairly rapid though deliberate. There must be no halting or jerkiness. In this way drawings of the circle, semicircle, quadrants, and other simple curves should be made.

The chalk should not be sharpened, unless it be cut in wedge form so that uniformity in breadth of line may be maintained.

Long, horizontal, vertical, and oblique parallel lines may be practised next, followed by simple geometrical forms, such as the square, rectangle, triangle, etc., and simple objects based on them. The course of Object Drawing described (Chap. VI., etc.) should then be followed.

22. Drawing in a Sitting Position.—Millboards or paper attached to them are kept in a nearly vertical position by means of a metal fastening, or the millboard passes through the slate-slot of the desk and rests on the bottom board of the locker. Sometimes the pengroove is deepened to take the lower edge of the millboard, which leans against a slate, book, or board wedged into the slate-slot.

Whichever method is adopted, extreme care should be taken that the drawing surface is within easy reach of the hand, so that the children do not assume a hurtful position when stretching across the intervening desk and that the arm is kept free of any support.

The drawing may be done with chalk, crayon, or short pieces of charcoal or lead pencil.

23. Drawing in Easel Fashion.—This is a valuable form of free drawing which differs from the generally adopted form of freearm drawing in that the arm is not extended. The board is supported on the knees and rests against the turned-back flap of the desk.

The objections to this method are that the feet require some support above the floor in order to raise the knees and board sufficiently, a want of rigidity of the drawing surface, and in the case of bigger children the cramped position of the arm, due to the proximity of the seat and desk. These difficulties are overcome where the desk and seat are not attached and there is a rail or support for the feet. The seat may then be set back at a convenient distance. This is undoubtedly an ideal method of drawing, whether in chalk or lead pencil, and is productive of light, free, and rapid work ; but it can only be carried out where sufficient floor space is available. A chair may take the place of the desk, the board resting against the back and the feet on the bottom rail.

For this method of free drawing with pencil, a short pencil should be used—about half a stick—held under the hand after the manner of chalk. Unlike ordinary free-hand drawing, the fingers are more rigid and the movement comes largely from the elbow. The tip of the little finger skims lightly over the paper and the wrist is moved freely.

Lines are drawn with very little pressure in long sweeping movements. The shoulder frequently comes into play, especially when drawing long lines.

24. Crayon Work.—*Materials and their Use.* Soft pastel crayons are recommended. They are very fragile, but small pieces may be used in crayon-holders.

Harder crayons in cedar wood do not break so easily, but require constant sharpening.

Coloured crayon is cleaner and less troublesome. than water-colour, but is only suitable for expressing "rough" truths of form and colour. It is a convenient medium for beginners and may be used for—

(*a*) Cultivating a light touch. The material easily breaks with rough handling.

(*b*) Giving elementary ideas of colour. Each child is supplied with a box, small bag or envelope, containing an assortment of crayons, including white and black, so that he may select the colour required. The names of the colours should be learnt. These should be restricted at first to the so-called primary colours, red, blue, and yellow.

In addition to outline drawing, crayons are specially useful for *mass drawing*. (See Art. 37.) White or tinted paper may be used, but rough brown paper is most suitable. The work may be applied to simple pattern, object, or nature drawing.

In pattern drawing variety in the same design can be produced by varying the direction and spacing of the crayon strokes.

The *secondary colours* must be obtained next from the primaries—thus, orange (red+yellow), violet (red+blue), green (blue+yellow). These may be produced in two ways—

(1) By lightly superimposing one colour on another in mass or line.

(2) By means of alternate parallel strokes of the primary colours. The distinct strokes of colour merge in the eye and produce the secondary. This method is more suitable for representing flat surfaces.

Selection of Tinted Paper.—This is important and should be subject to preliminary experiment on the part of the teacher or scholar. For outline drawings, the tint of the paper selected may approximate to that of the object to be drawn. Thus, in the drawing of a house, white crayon lines on red paper would represent brickwork, or the same paper would serve for a *surface drawing* of a carrot, flower-pot, etc., charcoal or black crayon being used to represent the dark portions and white crayon (used lightly) for the lighter tones. White metal, glassware, etc., may be represented by light strokes of white crayon on blue-grey paper.

In *Mass Drawing* careful consideration should be paid to the selection of the paper, so that its tint may harmonise with that of the drawing.

The paper may play an important part in the drawing in other ways; thus, it may be made to represent the lines dividing the different surfaces of an object, such as the petals and other parts of a flower ; or its tint may be made to modify the hue or the depth of tone by laying the crayon on lightly, or in open lines, so as not to obliterate that of the paper.

Beyond the Infant Stage, the laying on of a mass should be by means of a series of broad, parallel strokes (not necessarily open), as described in the chapter on Light and Shade. It must not be allowed to develop into an aimless scribble. Each stroke is a serious exercise in *drawing*.

Except in advanced work, which may be lightly set out in charcoal, the drawing should be laid on direct, working towards the outer edges. (See Arts. 36 and 37.) These need not be emphasized by means of a boundary line as in outline drawing, to which this method of portrayal is opposed.

Selected drawings may be cut out, mounted on paper or card of different tint by the child or teacher, and displayed in the class-room.

Simple effects of light and shade in this medium may be attempted at an early stage.

FREEHAND DRAWING.

25. Drawing on Slates.—On hygienic and other grounds the use of the slate is not to be recommended. Economy is the only point in its favour. Soft pencil or crayon should be used, the ordinary kinds being harsh and unyielding.

Slates ruled in squares are sometimes employed in Infant Schools, the grooved lines being used to run the pencil along. This practice is of little real value. The methods applying to the use of the slate pencil are the same as those for lead pencil.

26. Lead Pencil.—This is the medium most commonly used for drawing during and after school life. Properly used, the lead pencil lends itself to variety of expression. It should be soft (HB is the most useful degree) and of good quality. The point should be cut in long strokes, the lead, as a rule, being somewhat blunt. For *Freehand Drawing* the pencil should be long, anything less than half a stick being discarded.

27. Position of the Paper and Body.—The paper or drawing book must be placed squarely on the desk and never turned about. The left hand should rest lightly on the desk, keeping the paper or book in position. The body should be erect and the line of the shoulders kept parallel to the top edge of the paper.

28. Need of a Proper Method of Holding the Pencil.—In no branch of work is the effect of bad handling more evident than in pencil drawing. The deplorable practice of drawing in heavy dug-in lines, often indenting several sheets of paper at the same time, is difficult to eradicate.

The difficulty is due, probably, to the fact that the scholar has not completely separated the functions of the lead pencil as a *writing* and a *drawing* instrument. A glance round the class from the teacher's desk is often

DR.   2

sufficient to distinguish the good from the bad draughtsmen by the handling of the pencil.   When challenged, the
scholar usually assumes the correct position at once,
proving conclusively the need for continual supervision
until the correct position of the body and the movement
of the hand become more natural than the incorrect ones.

The process of *writing*, a form of drawing, is more or
less automatic.   The movements come mainly from the
fingers, the arm travels in one direction, the position of
the pen or pencil remaining constant.   In Freehand drawing the pencil assumes various directions and the movement comes mainly from the wrist.

29. How to Hold the Pencil.—The hand is turned
on its side, exposing the palm somewhat.   The pencil

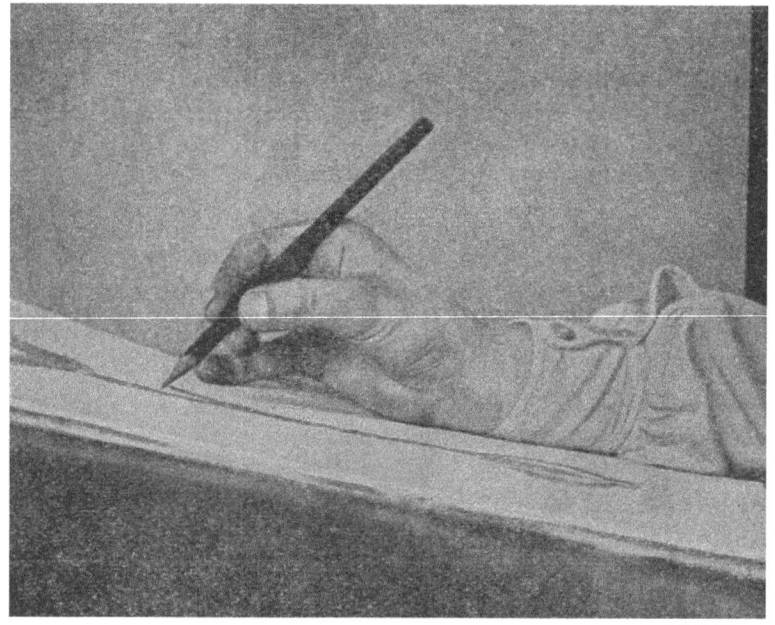

Fig. 1.

varies in direction according to the line to be drawn.   It
should be held firmly between the lower joints of the first
finger and the thumb and rest on the second finger about

two inches from the point. This distance will of course vary according to the size of the hand and the length of the line to be drawn. Thus the pencil will always assume a small angle with the paper and the *side* of the lead come in contact with it. The tip of the little finger should move freely over the paper. The pencil must not be held in the fork of the hand made by the first finger and the thumb.

Short, jerky strokes, sometimes spoken of as "rough sketching," must not be permitted. The pencil may be lifted from the paper, as occasion demands, in order *to continue* a line. Each stroke must be made with careful forethought, and, if necessary, after an imaginary line has been drawn in the required direction.

Finishing or " Lining in."—If the pencil be held in the manner described, a light grey line of uniform breadth will result. In the finishing stage all unnecessary lines should be removed. Should the drawing require strengthening, care must be taken to avoid a hard or wiry black line.

30. The Rubber should be soft. It must not be handled except when actually in use. The part to be used may be cleaned by rubbing on a corner of the paper.

Owing to its abuse the rubber has been abolished altogether in some schools. It should be used in moderation for the removal of incorrect drawing only *after* the line has been redrawn satisfactorily. Where too free use of the rubber is made, as a disciplinary measure its use may be prohibited, or allowed only at the end of the lesson.

31. Squared Paper is not generally to be recommended. If employed at all, its use should be restricted to the lowest classes. The squares should be of a faint grey tone of not less than one inch. Squares made up of straight lines are best for straight line practice, while squares indicated by dots at the angles are suitable for curved forms.

The advantage of the use of squared paper is that it provides a basis to work upon. The length and direction of lines to be drawn can be easily determined before the actual drawing, so that the child's mind may be devoted entirely to the execution.   The lines should be drawn their full length without hesitation.

Squared paper is suited principally for freehand and brushwork practice in the simple elements of form ;

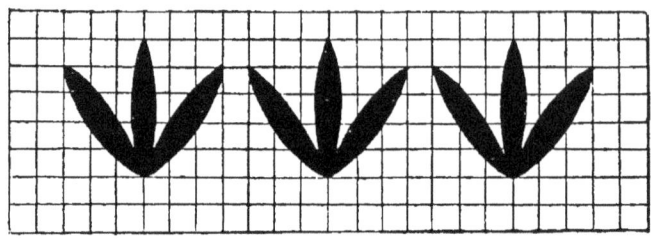

Fig. 2.

thus, by repetition, reversal, or alternation of straight or curved lines, repeating patterns or representations of simple objects may be produced (Fig. 2).

Fig. 3.   Fig. 4.   Fig. 5.

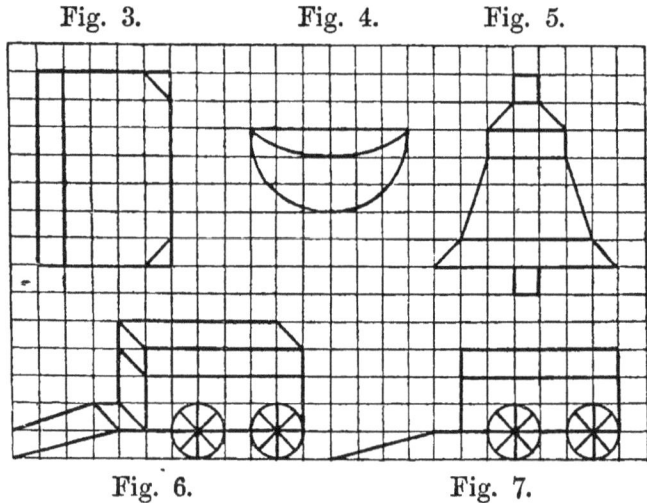

Fig. 6.   Fig. 7.

Simple objects drawn in elevation (Figs. 3, 4, 7) form interesting exercises, but should not be continued long, as the judgment of proportion is not exercised sufficiently thereby.   Copies conveying false ideas of perspective (Fig. 6), or in which curves are falsely represented by straight lines (Fig. 5), *must be avoided.*

CHAPTER III.

SOME METHODS OF HAND AND EYE TRAINING.

The first endeavours of a young painter must be employed in the attainment of mechanical dexterity.
SIR JOSHUA REYNOLDS.

[The following methods may be applied to drawing in any medium.]

32. Imaginary Drawing.—This term has been adopted to describe the practice in the various movements necessary in order to obtain facility in handling the chalk, crayon and pencil, or to discern and memorise a form previous to actually drawing it.

The exercises should be taken at the beginning of the lesson for a few minutes, the form selected being the basis of the example of the drawing lesson to follow.

The teacher faces the class and describes the movement *in the air* with the *left* hand. The children make a similar movement simultaneously, using the *right* hand, and with the same medium. It is an advantage if the teacher draw against a vertical sheet of glass, such as that of a model of the Picture Plane, placed between him and the class. This apparatus is extremely useful when conducting exercises in Eye Training.

EYE TRAINING EXERCISES.

33. Direction of Line.—Concrete examples should be employed for preference from the very beginning. Thus, a hoop suspended against the wall facing the class will serve for practice in circular movements. The hand should describe a " covering line " in the air, moving towards the left and right in turn.

Similarly, a map-pole, long laths, edges of frames, cupboards, etc., will provide practice in imaginary drawing of straight lines. It will be necessary to train the child to close the left eye during this practice, and such training will be found of great advantage at a later stage. The line should now be drawn, no correction or erasure being permitted. The lines should be repeated again and again until a satisfactory drawing is obtained.

34. Proportion.—Exercises must be devised for comparing measurements of objects at sight.

(a) Lengths measured in the same direction; *e.g.* vertical with vertical, horizontal with horizontal.

(b) Lengths measured in different directions; *e.g.* horizontal with vertical, or either with oblique.

Interesting examples must be employed in order to prevent these exercises becoming monotonous. Thus, for comparative measurements along the same straight line bands or loops of bright coloured paper, ribbon, or wool might be attached to a lath or pole, or small flags attached to pins might be stuck at required intervals. For other measurements, objects such as a pen, pointer, or walking-stick might be employed.

When drawing, the method of procedure should be varied; sometimes all the objects to be drawn may be exhibited at once, side by side on the same level, or on different levels; or the objects may be set up and drawn in turn, making the first the standard of measurement for others.

35. Fractional Method of Measurement.—The eye must be trained to judge and record measurements accurately. It is not necessary, however, nor is it generally desirable that the children should state the proportions of an object arithmetically.

The method of estimating the length of one line by means of exact multiples of another frequently fails in practice. Glaring errors in proportion (easily discovered at sight by the child himself when challenged) are frequent even after he has employed this method. On the other hand, he would probably unhesitatingly give the comparative lengths of two pieces of *sugarstick* without such aid.

36. Mass as an Aid in the Judgment of Proportion. —Exercises in linear measurement should not be continued long without consideration of *area*.

The representation of forms by their outlines is a convention. We see objects in *masses* and we get a more faithful representation of their proportions by dealing with them as such. Chalk, crayon, and brush drawing are admirably adapted to this method of treatment.

37. Direct Mass Drawing.—The drawing is begun at the *centre* of the mass and made to grow outward by means of spiral movements, the outline being drawn *last*. Or broad chalk or brush strokes are laid alternately on either side of a central stroke or line.

This method is peculiarly adapted to brushwork, and is further described in the section of the book dealing with this subject. It is also suited for freearm drawing in chalk, crayon, or pencil, being applied best to objects that are represented in the main by circular, elliptical, or oval forms.

Beginners usually attach too much importance to the representation of detail—small features loom large in their mind's eye. Thus, in drawing a box, the tiniest rivet is sometimes made to assume the proportions of a large nail-head.

Direct mass drawing is a valuable corrective and means

of training the judgment as to the comparative values of the parts of an object. The scholar is compelled to seize on the main forms and deal with them before the subsidiary ones. Mechanical use of construction lines is avoided. This method cannot be applied with advantage beyond the elementary stage when the need for careful setting-out of a drawing will usually arise.

38. Mass-filling.—A form previously drawn in outline is filled-in with chalk, pencil, or colour.

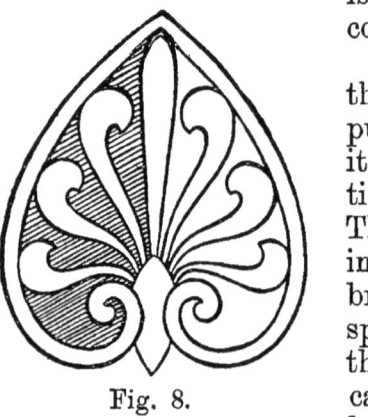

Fig. 8.

This is of most value where the drawing is intended for the purpose of demonstration and it is sought to emphasise particular shapes or proportions. Thus, in the symmetrical drawing (Fig. 8), the proportionate breadth of the forms and the spaces between them as well as the exact nature of the curves can be appreciated better in the left half of the copy, where the background has been filled in, than in the right half.

39. "Cut-out" Forms.—The following method has been found very useful for demonstrating form by the aid of mass. Large shapes, symmetrical and otherwise, are cut out of stiff white or light tinted paper and set up as drawing examples. The copies can be cut easily to any size and in any number. They are in absolute silhouette. They interest the children, especially if they watch the teacher "make them."

Thus a piece of paper ABCD (Fig. 9), not less than 12″ square, is doubled along the line EF and a simple shield form produced by a single cut along the curve AE. The shield form (Fig. 10) is pinned to the blackboard and shows white on black, while the portion of paper cut away may also be pinned alongside and below a chalk line, giving a duplicate copy in silhouette, Fig. 11.

Occasionally the copy may be presented in stages to be drawn by the children. Thus, the square or rectangle is

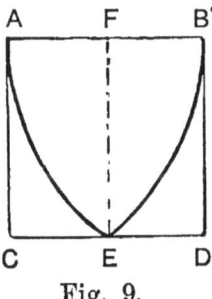
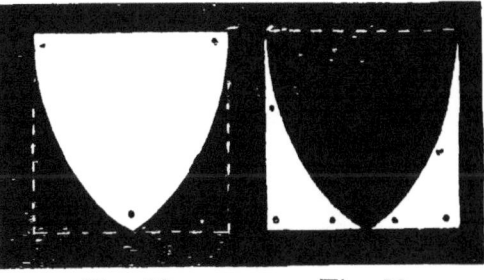

Fig. 9.   Fig. 10.   Fig. 11.

pinned on the board and drawn by the children, and the next stage of the desired form, say, a shield cut out of a similar piece of paper, pinned beside it. The evolution of the form would thus be shown at a glance. The idea may be developed further, especially where freehand practice in ornament is desired ; thus a double square of paper cut four-fold will produce forms such as Figs. 12 and 13.

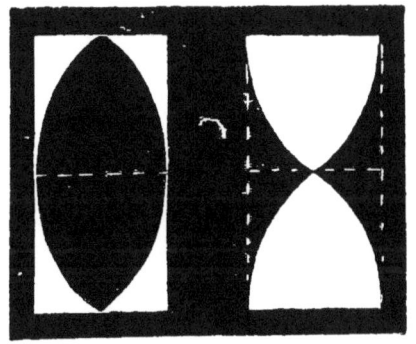

Fig. 12.   Fig. 13.

Further development of shield forms is shown in Figs. 14-17. These suggest another type of " copy," viz. patterns cut out in coloured

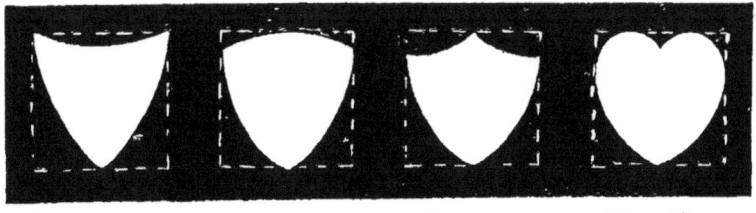

Fig. 14.   Fig. 15.   Fig. 16.   Fig. 17.

paper and mounted on cards. Small examples may be made and distributed for drawing.

40. Leaf forms may be cut in the same way to any desired scale and the development from simple to compound shapes shown stage by stage in double process. Thus, Fig 18, A and B show the cut-out portions in two

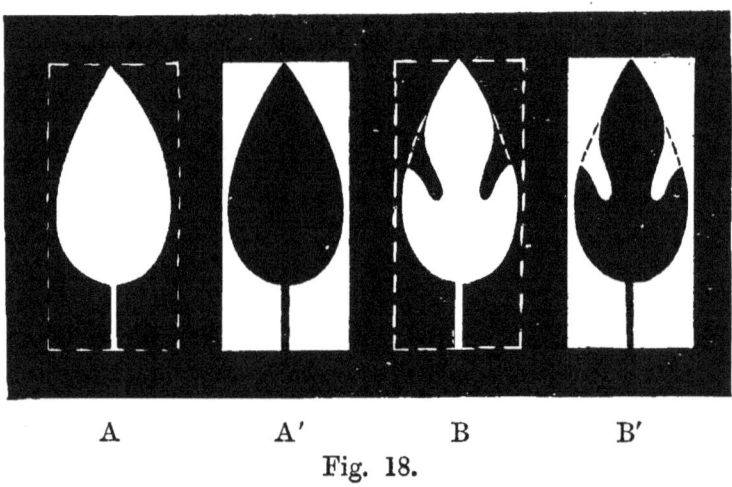

A   A'   B   B'

Fig. 18.

stages in white on black, while A', B' show the corresponding remainders producing the pattern black on white. The small portions cut out in Fig. B are pinned to B' at *x, y*. Smaller details, *e.g.* serrations of leaves, can be illustrated on a large scale in a similar manner. Interior markings, such as the veins of leaves, may be added sometimes in charcoal or chalk.

Natural leaves, pressed and mounted on cards form very useful exercises, and may be classified according to their shape ; *e.g.* lancet or cordate forms, smooth-edged or serrated-edged, simple and compound leaves.

The leaves should be gathered in autumn, pressed between sheets of blotting paper, and then gummed on cards.

HAND TRAINING EXERCISES.

The movements explained in the following notes should be practised by means of Imaginary drawing as described in Art. 32.

41. Method of Holding Chalk and Pencil.—*In Free-arm* drawing with chalk, the latter is held inside the hand irrespective of the direction of the line to be drawn.

In Freehand or pencil drawing, the pencil should invariably assume a direction *at right angles to the line to be drawn*, whether straight or curved.

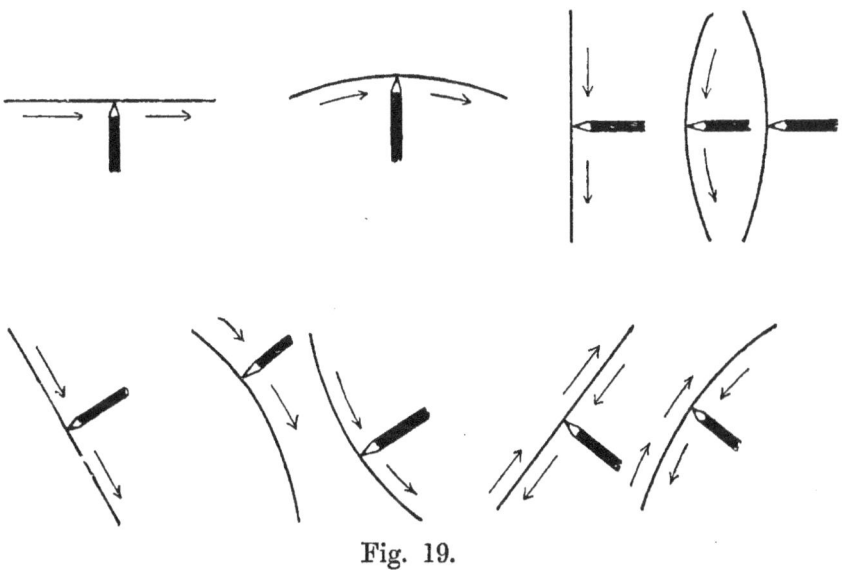

Fig. 19.

In the accompanying diagrams (Fig. 19), the small arrows indicate the *direction* in which the respective lines are to be drawn. The position of the pencil is also shown.

42. Rules for Drawing Straight or Curved Lines, Freehand and Freearm.

(*a*) Straight or curved lines in a **horizontal** direction should always be drawn from left to right. In Freearm drawing, curves may be swung either way.

(*b*) Straight or curved lines in a **vertical** or **inclined** direction should be begun, as a rule, at the upper extremity. *Those slanting upwards towards the right*, however, may be begun from either extremity according to convenience (see Fig. 19).

(*c*) **The Circle and Ellipse** (Figs. 20) in *Freearm* drawing should be drawn without the aid of construction lines, or, at most, light, short strokes should mark the

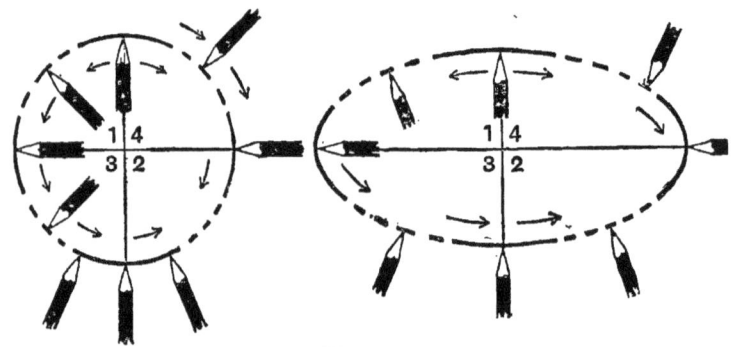

Fig. 20.

extreme height and width. The form should then be described in the air and finally drawn with an easy swinging movement.

In *Freehand* drawing of these forms, two diameters only, horizontal and vertical, may be drawn by way of construction. The extremities of these lines should be "rounded" first in order to avoid angularity at these points. Arrows pointing in opposite directions indicate that the particular portion of the curve may be drawn in either direction.

The *quadrants* are numbered in order of difficulty in drawing, the last being the most difficult. Curves are easier to draw with pencil when the latter can be held *inside* them, and they should be drawn thus as far as the bending of the hand on the wrist will comfortably-permit.

In order to cultivate flexibility of the wrist, curves should be practised in various positions at an early stage, and extreme care must be taken that children do not escape this necessary training by turning their papers or bodies about.

PLATE I.

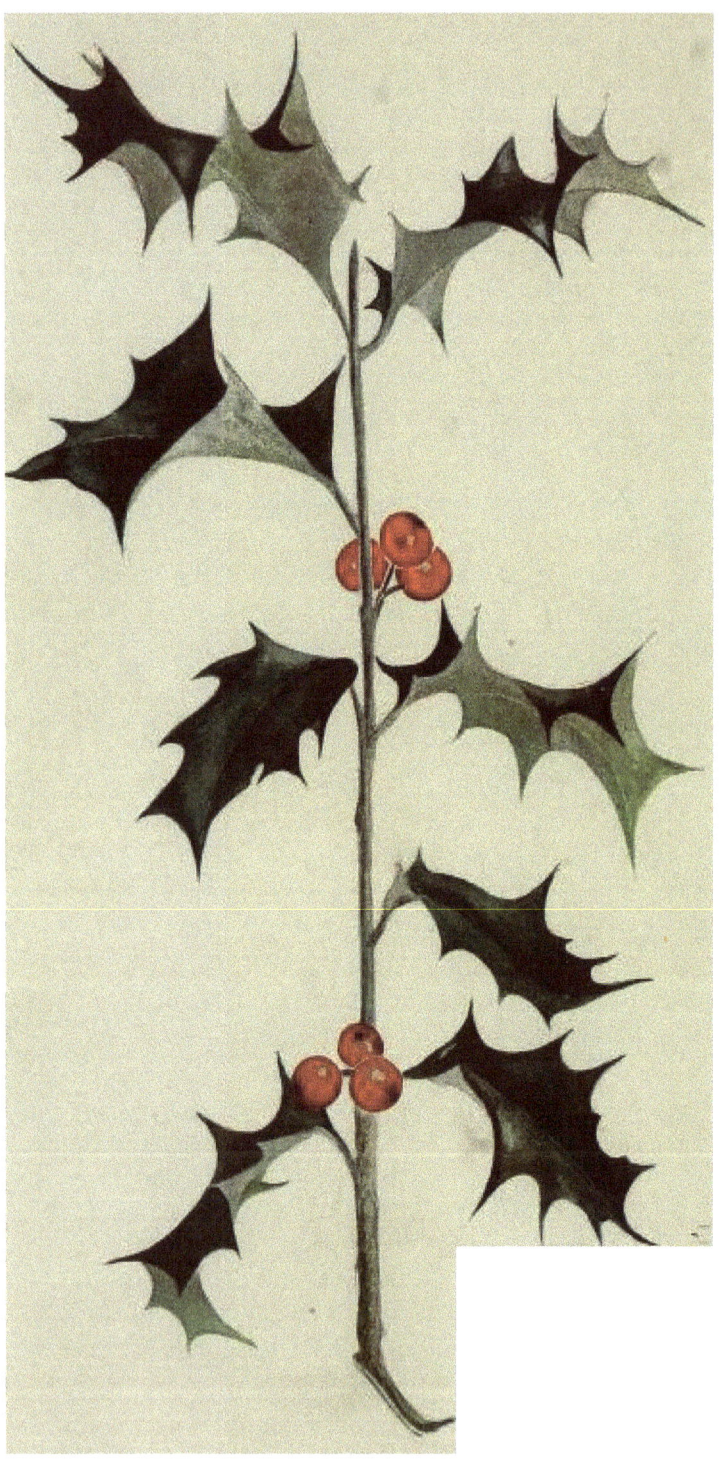

CHAPTER IV.

BRUSHWORK AND COLOUR STUDY.

If you can match a colour accurately and lay it delicately, you are a painter, as, if you can strike a note surely, and deliver it clearly, you are a singer. You may then choose what you will paint, or what you will sing.—RUSKIN.

43. Its Importance and Value.—The complete representation of an object involves the study of colour. This study is of fascinating interest to the youngest child, and should be included in the Drawing Syllabus throughout the school period. The brush is a " broader " instrument of expression than the pencil—more subtle and expressive. It encourages bold and rapid work and at the same time is suitable for the most delicate drawing.

44. Special Difficulties.—The brush needs greater control than the pencil, hence a considerable amount of practice in manipulation is required. Wrong methods of holding and using the brush are difficult to eradicate, therefore the need of more individual teaching from the beginning. The materials required increase as the pupil makes progress, hence more time is necessary in preparation and distribution.

45. Materials for Brushwork.

Water Colours.—Hard cake colours require time to rub down.

Dyes and inks are unsatisfactory; the colours are crude, do not mix well, and do not take well to paper.

Moist colours in tubes are most convenient. It is an advantage in the early stages especially to restrict the colours to Gamboge, Prussian Blue, and Crimson Lake.

29

Chinese White may be used to make a body colour for use on brown or tinted paper. Colour boxes containing eight to twelve colours may be used for more advanced work.

Brushes.—The most suitable brush for ordinary exercises is No. 5 or 6 camel or Siberian hair. In later stages two or three sable brushes, Nos. 3, 5, and 6, will be useful,

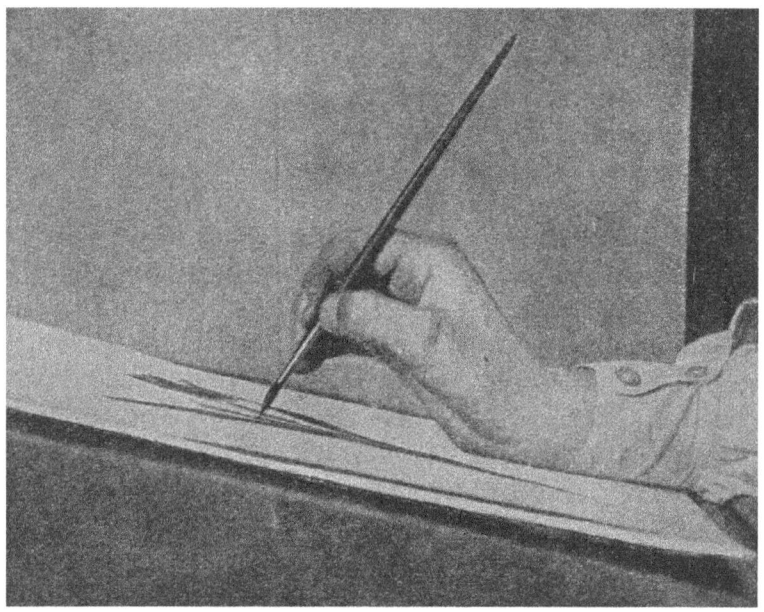

Fig. 21.
First Method of holding the Brush.

since it is often convenient to have two or three brushes in use at the same time. Brushes must be kept clean; they should be washed after each lesson and carefully stored. The hair should be brought to a fine point and not allowed to be bent when drying. It is a good plan to keep them in a large jar, handles downward.

Palettes.—Ordinary round china palettes, into which prepared colour may be poured, can be used in first stages.

For pupils who mix their own colour a china palette with six divisions is recommended; the three lower for colours squeezed direct from the tube, the upper divisions for mixing.

Water Glasses.—Wide shallow vessels, not easily upset, are necessary.

Blotting Paper or Clean Rag, to soak up superfluous paint. Brushes must not be placed in the mouth; it is a dangerous practice.

Teachers' Materials for Demonstration.—Hogshair or red sable brush, large, round, and well pointed. Whiting for blackboard; this must be made thick or will run down. Special prepared water colour, opaque or transparent,

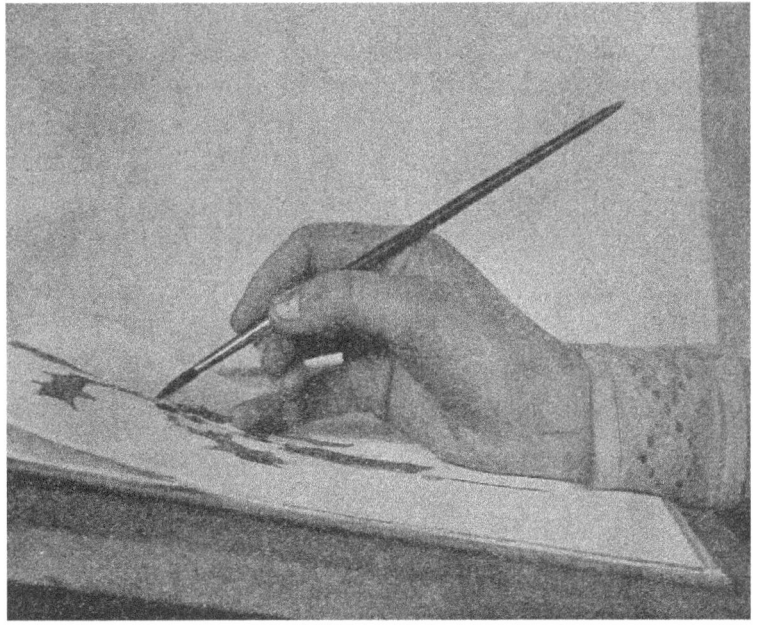

Fig. 22.
Second Method of holding the Brush.

usually sold in tins. The ordinary tube colours mixed rather thicker serve very well, but care must be taken that the brush is not overloaded or the colour will be unmanageable.

46. Brushwork.—(*a*) "*Blobbing,*" or making impressions with the side of the brush. An attempt is made to represent forms by repetition of "blobs," and various designs consisting of strokes and brush impressions are patterned on squared paper. This method gives the pupil some idea of manipulating the brush, but the repetition of meaningless forms is uneducational.

(b) *Direct Brush-drawing* of simple natural and artificial objects. This method is very popular in Infants' Schools and the lower classes of Upper Schools. It should be followed in the higher classes by water-colour painting.

47. Stage I.*—The colours are mixed by the teacher and may be stored in well-corked bottles. One colour only is used for each object.

Brush practice.—The brush must be held near the upper end of ferrule, and should slant in the same direction as the stroke about to be made. The guidance may be entirely from the wrist and forearm, as in Fig. 21, or may be assisted by the little finger, as in Fig. 22.

Straight strokes (a) even in thickness, (b) wider in centre.

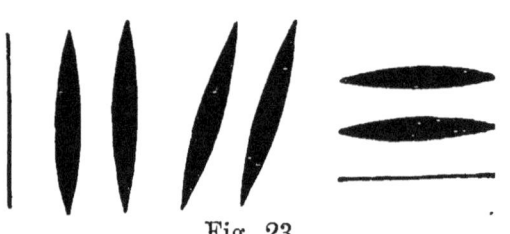

Fig. 23.

A few minutes only, at the beginning of each lesson, should be given to strokes. They should be at least three times the size of this illustration.

Curved strokes (a) even in thickness, (b) wider in centre.

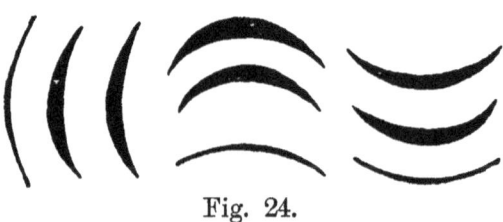

Fig. 24.

These strokes should be practised in all positions with varying curvature and size. Squared paper may be used in the first exercises.

Simple leaf forms (using above strokes).—Snowdrop buds and leaves, seeds of ash tree, blades of grass, crocus, mistletoe, etc.; see Fig. 25.

* See Preface with regard to the meaning of the term *Stage.*

Other simple natural forms.—Sprouting onion, carnation cutting, roots of various kinds, twigs and branches.

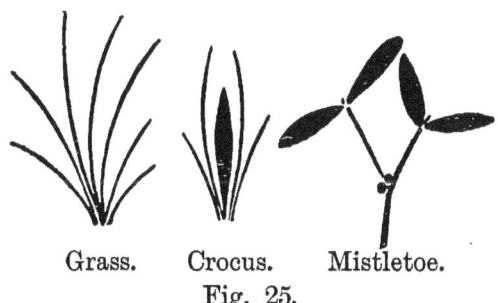

Grass.   Crocus.   Mistletoe.
Fig. 25.

Objects in Outline.—In order to cultivate a light touch artificial objects and natural forms, such as mentioned in Art. 61, can be drawn in outline with the point of the brush.

48. Stage II.—Colour mixed by the teacher as before.

Brush strokes.—Spindle strokes as in Stage I., and strokes with one side straight.

The latter can be made more easily by concentrating the attention on the straight side.

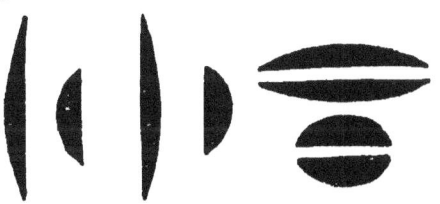

Fig. 26.

Leaf forms, omitting serrations.—Each leaf to be made with two strokes only. The veins may be indicated either

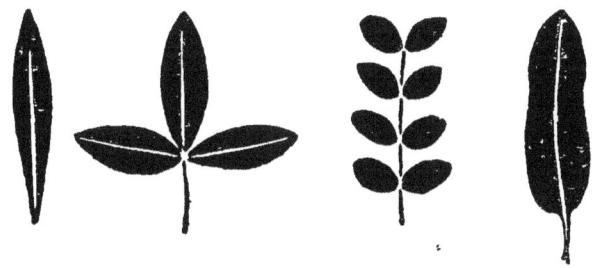

Wall-flower.   Laburnum.   Privet.   Laurel.
Fig. 27.

by leaving a thin line between the strokes, which should,

however, meet at the point of the leaf, or by allowing the second stroke to overlap the first.

Wall-flower, laburnum, privet, laurel, rose, berberry, ash, acacia, etc. (see Fig. 27).

Berries.—A spot of paint on the paper is worked by the brush into the desired shape. Hawthorn, wild rose, snowberry, woody nightshade, lily of the valley seeds, etc.

49. Stage III.—Colours mixed by pupils. (For method see Art. 52.)

Brush strokes as before, together with *tapering strokes.*

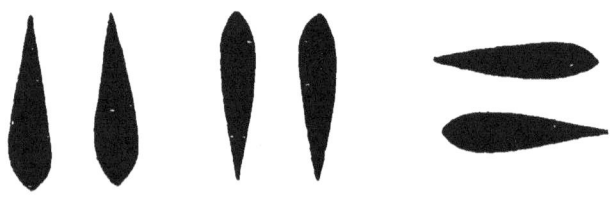

Fig. 28.

Leaf and petal forms, omitting serrations.—Restrict the brush strokes to four for each leaf.

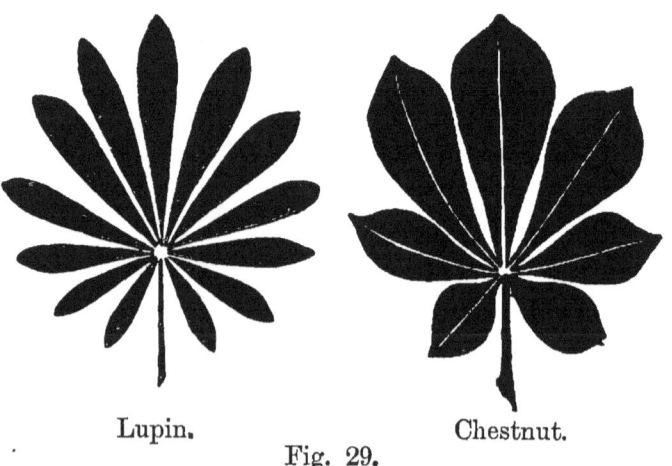

Lupin.   Chestnut.

Fig. 29.

Lupin, chestnut, virginia creeper, daisy, yew, mimosa, box, etc. (Figs. 29 and 30).

Note.—In the first three stages the chief object is to gain control of the brush. The forms should not be worked up by many brush touches, but should be boldly made in the fewest possible strokes. These stages must be looked upon simply as preliminary brush exercises leading to more valuable work in the higher stages. The brush strokes are omitted from some good schemes of work but they have been found valuable when used in moderation.

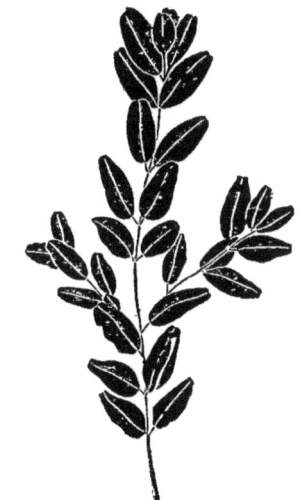

Box Leaves.
Fig. 30.

50. Stages IV., V., and VI.—*Painting without outline.* In these stages follow the Syllabuses for Nature and Object Drawing.

Hints.—Use fairly thick colour and see that brush is well pointed.

When an object exhibits two or three different colours (*e.g.* an apple may show a combination of red, yellow, and green tints), it is advisable to mix and match the shades in separate palettes, and then by using three brushes to paint the whole object while the colour is wet. In this way the colours will blend naturally.

In the case of a leaf or fruit which exhibits spots or edges of different colours these may be dotted on the ground colour while it is wet. In painting flowers, paint alternate petals, so that they may dry and not run together.

51. Painting.—This includes the scientific study of colour and the filling in of a previously drawn copy.

Flat-tinting or Washing : filling a given space with even colour.

Directions for First Exercise.—Prepare a rectangle, about 4½″ by 2½″, choose a pale colour (gamboge) and mix a light tint. (Paper to be placed on a slightly sloping desk).

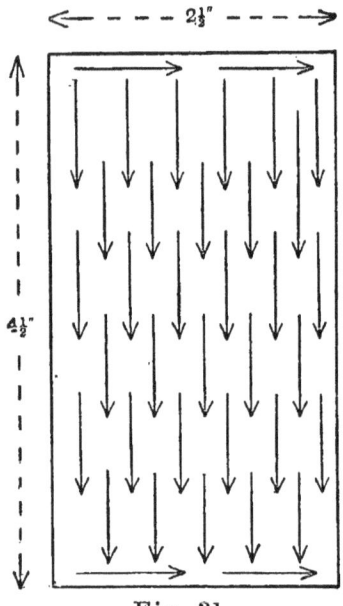

Fig. 31.

Take a brushful of paint and, beginning at the top left-hand corner, draw along top edge with the point of brush; then paint with downward brush-strokes, but move from left to right and back again, as in diagram. Hold the brush nearly upright, keep it well supplied with colour, and see that the handle always takes the same direction as the strokes.

Guide the brush carefully at the edges, taking care that the paint does not go outside.

One row of brush-strokes must not be allowed to dry before the next row is painted, or a dark streak will appear where the colour overlaps.

If too much paint is left at the end, wipe or squeeze the brush not too dry and allow it to absorb colour. Keep colour well stirred.

Do not retouch in any way. The whole surface may be repainted when dry, but an even tone cannot be produced by retouching parts.

Suitable Exercises in flat-tinting.—Freehand copies of ornament and original designs; maps and geographical diagrams; plans and elevations in solid geometry; scientific diagrams, etc.

The light and shade on common objects, such as the box (Fig. 110), may be expressed in varying tones of the same colour.

Very effective results may be obtained by flat-tinting over shaded pencil drawings.

52. More Advanced Painting.—Natural and artificial objects in natural colours.

Colour Charts.—The necessary diagrams should be previously prepared with compass and ruler. Colours required:—Red, blue, and yellow.

(1) In this chart each circle is covered with flat wash and allowed to dry. The colours overlap and make new colours.

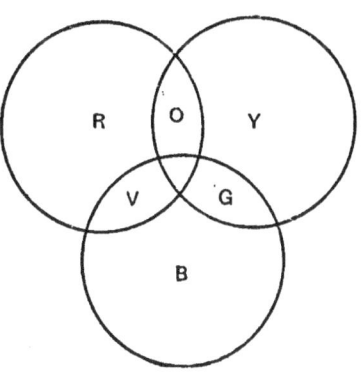

Fig. 32.

(2) Washes of yellow, blue, and red are painted in alternate spaces. The colours are then mixed in palette,

Yellow and blue = green,   Blue and red = violet,

Yellow and red = orange,

and remaining spaces are filled.

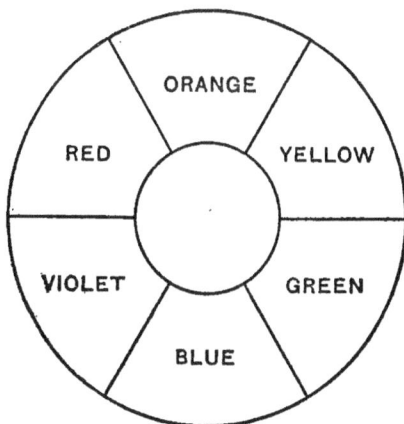

Fig. 33.

(3) The natural order of colours may be discovered by studying the rainbow, and the sky at sunset. The scholars should watch for these phenomena and make a diagram indicating the order of the colours they see (Fig. 34).

The experiment of splitting up a ray of white light into its constituent colours by means of a glass prism will reveal the same order and may be introduced at this stage. The prism is held between a ray of sunlight and a piece of white paper.

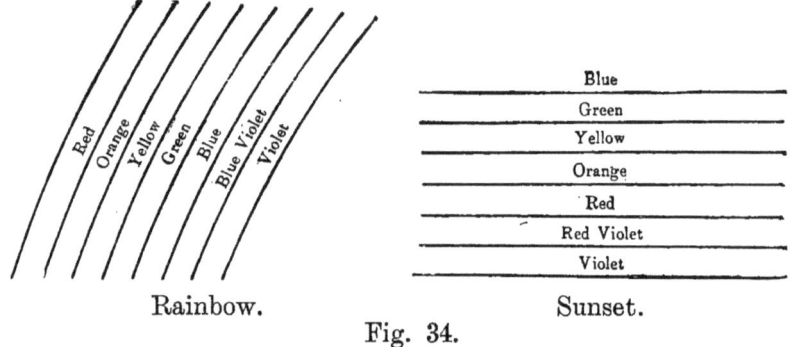

Rainbow.   Sunset.

Fig. 34.

The chart (Fig. 35) is arranged in similar order. The complementary colours are opposite each other ; thus violet is opposite to yellow and is said to be **complementary,** because it contains the remaining colours, red and blue.

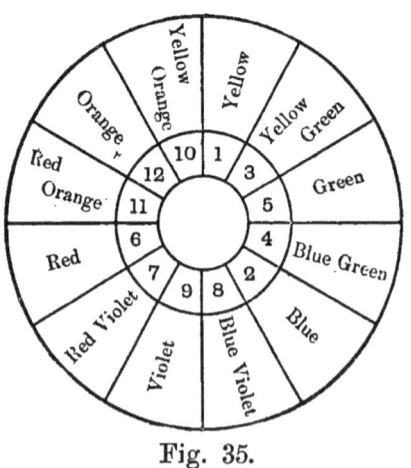

Fig. 35.

If the colours are mixed in the following order an even gradation will be secured.

Yellow and Blue.
{
1. Yellow.
2. Blue.
3. Yellow Green (place small quantity of Blue in Yellow).
4. Blue Green (place small quantity of Yellow Green in Blue).
5. Green (mix Blue Green and Yellow Green).
}

PLATE II.

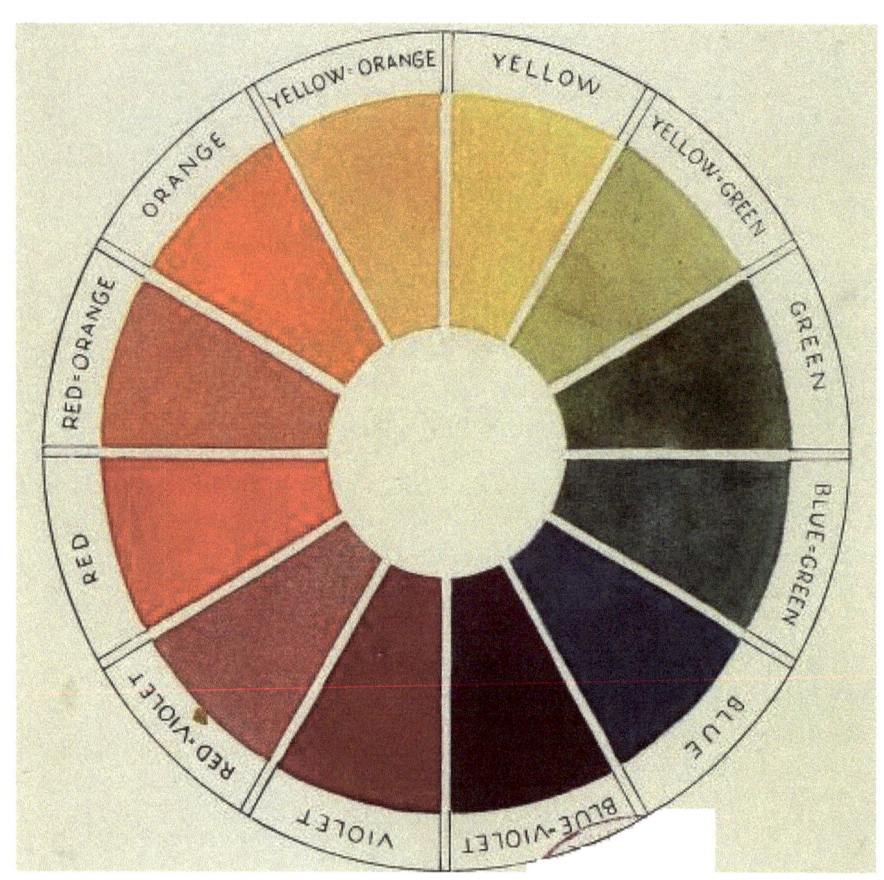

COLOUR CHART.

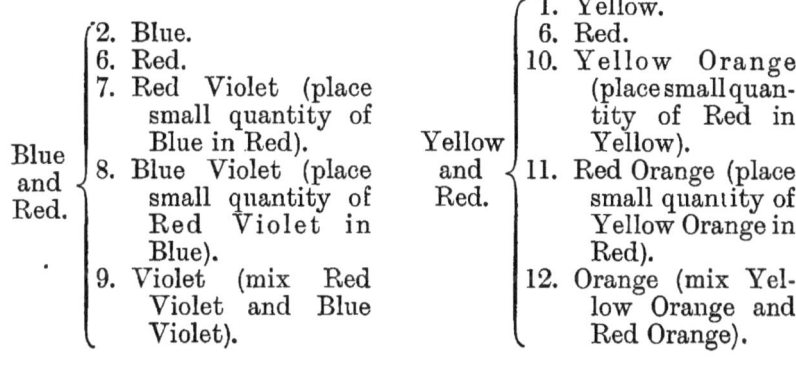

Blue
and
Red.
{
2. Blue.
6. Red.
7. Red Violet (place small quantity of Blue in Red).
8. Blue Violet (place small quantity of Red Violet in Blue).
9. Violet (mix Red Violet and Blue Violet).
}

Yellow
and
Red.
{
1. Yellow.
6. Red.
10. Yellow Orange (place small quantity of Red in Yellow).
11. Red Orange (place small quantity of Yellow Orange in Red).
12. Orange (mix Yellow Orange and Red Orange).
}

See Plate II.

53. Exercises in Matching Colours.

Before painting leaves, flowers, and other objects the colour must be matched on a "trial" paper, which is held near the object and submitted for the teacher's approval.

In mixing colours place darker colours into the lighter. Thus, in making green, place blue into yellow.

The colours may be softened and more nearly approximated to nature by adding a *little* complementary colour. Thus the green of nature contains some red.

54. Tone Values in Colour.—All colours in nature exhibit a gradation in tone. This gradation is not always evident to the unpractised eye, but must be taken into account if we are to represent the colours of natural objects with some truth and feeling. There are several methods of expressing this gradation in colour which can only be used by experienced artists, but the following is suitable for beginners and can be extended to any degree of accuracy. (A palette of six divisions is necessary.)

A sheet of paper is prepared as in diagram. A little colour from the tube is placed in one division of palette, water in the remaining divisions. A very light tint of the colour is mixed in No. 1 division of palette and painted evenly in corresponding rectangle. No. 2 is made a little deeper and painted in No. 2 rectangle, No. 3 deeper still, and so on until we have five tints of the same colour arranged in due order. Mix a good quantity of each; it will be difficult to match the tint if it is exhausted before

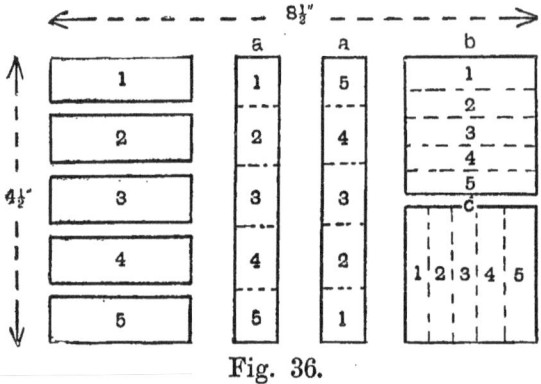

Fig. 36.

the exercise is complete. Now if these tints are in an even scale we may proceed to blend them as follows:—A small brushful of No. 1 is taken and one-fifth of rectangle *a* is coloured, the brush is then dipped into No. 2 and stirred, and while colour is wet the 2nd fifth of space is painted, the brush is then dipped in No. 3, stirred, and while colour is wet the 3rd fifth is coloured, and so on. Other spaces such as *b* and *c* can be coloured in same way, and the exercise should be repeated until an even gradation of tone is obtained. By taking more tints the gradation becomes more refined. A gradation in hue is effected by using two different colours.

Drawings of rounded objects can be tinted in this way to show light and shade effects.

55. Hints on Painting a Spray from Nature, *e.g.* the holly (Plate I.) and rose-spray (Plate III.).

Draw lightly in outline; use rubber very sparingly.

Note the main effects of light and shade and the corresponding gradations of colour. Mark the outlines of very high lights, which should be left unpainted or at least painted only in the lightest tint. Mix two or three separate shades for each leaf, petal or berry. Great care

PLATE III.

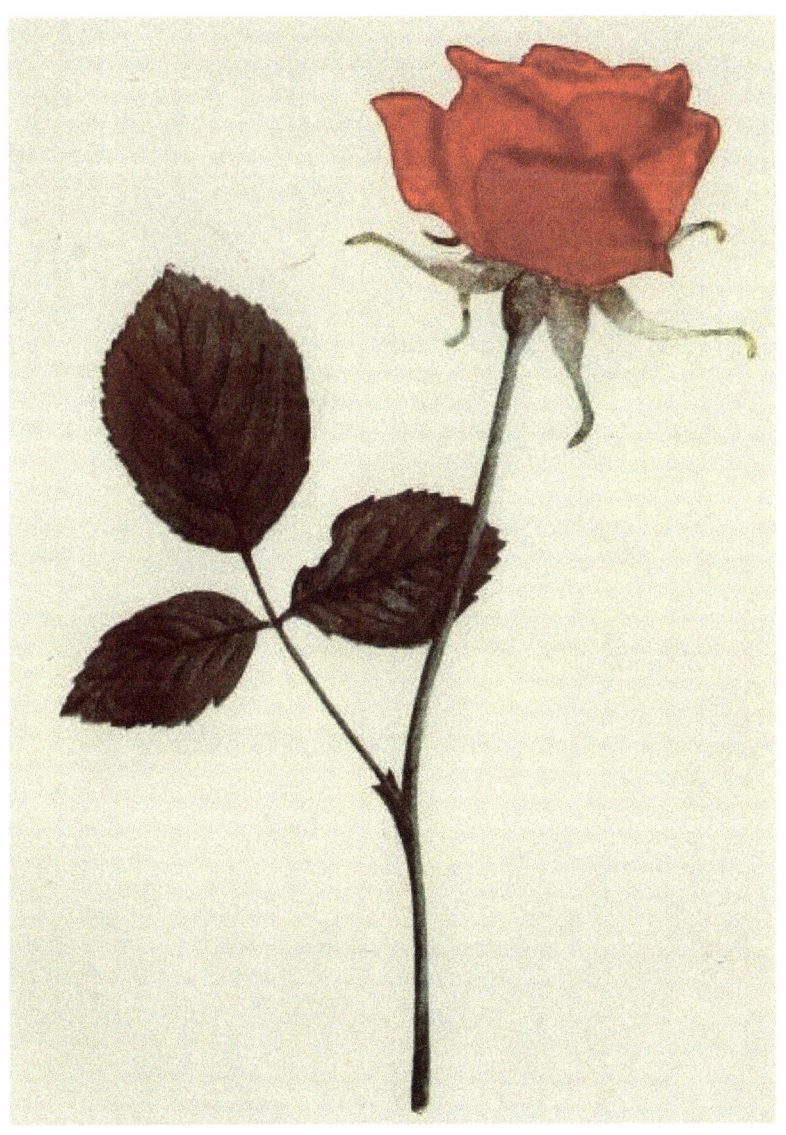

must be used in order to match the shades as nearly as possible. The colours of flowers, leaves, and stalks will harmonize more satisfactorily if each partakes of the colour of the others—thus in the case of the rose-spray a little carmine or crimson lake should be added to the green for the leaves and stalk. Very effective results are produced by mixing the colours on the actual drawing, but this method requires considerable skill and is consequently not so suitable for beginners.

Study the general effect of a leaf or petal and paint with disregard of smaller veins and other details.

Use two or three brushes, one for each tone. Try to paint the whole of a given space while the colour is wet.

When the first coat is dry proceed to repaint smaller spaces in the same way.

Shadow or background may be coloured by mixing all the colours used and diluting with water.

Note.—The Coloured Plates are reproductions of work by pupils who have followed the exercises here explained.

CHAPTER V.

NATURE DRAWING.

I would rather teach Drawing that my pupils may learn to love Nature, than teach the looking at Nature that they may learn to draw.—RUSKIN.

56. Reasons for Teaching.—All our ideas of beauty are derived from Nature.

Knowledge gained firsthand by the pupil's own observation and experience is the most valuable.

The simplest natural object gives scope of expression to the youngest scholar and is worthy of the greatest artist.

Delight in Nature is increased; pleasure in life ever widened and refined.

Works of Art—decorative and pictorial—appeal more and more to the interest of a well-trained pupil, who is thus enabled to continue his education on a broader basis.

DRAWING FOR INFANTS.

57. Characteristics of Young Children.—In making a syllabus for Nature Drawing the following characteristics of young children must be considered.

Love of activity. Every child should be supplied with a real object, since ideas of form and size are gained as much by sense of feeling as of sight. Knowledge gained by seeing, tasting, smelling, and handling may be made more exact and lasting by drawing.

Powers of observation and expression very limited. The teacher must be satisfied if child is able to express some truth; the amount of truth will increase with child's development. It is important always to see the good points; praise rather than blame.

Control of hand very imperfect. Small drawings and drawings of details should not be required. Large drawings in chalk and crayon on small blackboards or tinted paper and direct colour studies with brush are suitable at this stage. Free-arm and mass drawing should be the chief methods employed (see Chaps. II. and III.).

Inability to give sustained attention. Lessons must be short; they will be of greater interest if closely connected with other subjects of the curriculum. Children should be encouraged to bring their own specimens; they should learn to name the leaves, plants and trees. The teacher may increase interest by explaining in a general way the nature, growth and use of the various objects.

58. Suitable Lessons.

Leaves.	*Flowers.*	*Fruits.*	*Vegetables.*	*Pictures.*
Laurel	Crocus	Apple	Carrot	*Introducing—*
Aucuba	Tulip	Pear	Turnip	Trees
Lime	Daisy	Orange	Beetroot	Grass
Poplar	Snowdrop	Lemon	Cucumber	Mountains
Laburnum	Etc.	Banana	Broadbean	Sea
Clover		Cherry	Radish	Sun
Mistletoe		Plum	Etc.	Moon
Etc.		Etc.		Etc.

59. Methods of Teaching.—The natural objects to be studied are distributed—one specimen to each child if possible—and teacher questions class as to form, colour, etc. The children are allowed to give information of any kind concerning the object, such as where it grows, what it is used for, etc. The teacher summarises this information and proceeds to question on best method of drawing. During the lesson individual children are assisted, errors are pointed out, and general mistakes illustrated on blackboard. At end of lesson all drawings are shown for teacher's inspection and the best selected for praise. The more advanced pupils will take much pleasure in using scissors to cut out their drawings. Drawings of leaves on green paper treated in this way are very effective if mounted on white paper; the teacher may undertake to do this as a reward for the best work.

DRAWING FOR OLDER SCHOLARS.

60. Considerations in making a Syllabus of Lessons.

Exercises should be arranged to suit the season of the year and such natural objects should be selected that every child can be supplied with a specimen. In winter pressed leaves on cards and photographs may be used.

Lessons must be carefully graduated. If the exercises are too easy, the pupil loses interest; if too difficult, he loses confidence as well.

The same objects should be expressed in several ways. By varying the media the characteristics are brought out. Some objects owe their beauty mainly to form, others to colour, and others to the effect of light and shade.

Nature study should be a prominent feature. Pupils should learn the names and uses of the objects they draw; they should be able to identify leaves, flowers, trees, etc.

Similar objects should be studied together for the purpose of comparison and contrast, *e.g.*

Ash and acacia leaves	Harebell and bluebell
Sycamore and plane leaves	Orange and lemon
Chestnut and virginia creeper leaves	Apple and pear

61. Stages I. and II.—Simple natural objects without perspective.

Leaves.		*Buds.*	*Flowers.*
Bay	Plantain	Crocus	Crocus
Laurel	Willow	Snowdrop	Tulip
Aucuba	Almond	Rose	Clematis
Lilac	Cornel	Convolvulus	Pansy
Privet	Camellia	Tulip	Snowdrop
Clover	Laburnum	Poppy	Poppy
Rubber	Mistletoe	Harebell	Etc.
Etc.	Etc.	Etc.	

Fruits.	Vegetables.	Berries.	Seeds.
Cherry	Carrot	Acorn	Poppyhead
Pear	Onion	Hawthorn	Sycamore
Apple	Turnip	Wild rose	Pea pod
Orange	Radish	Berberry	Chestnut
Lemon	Cucumber	Oak galls	Walnut
Gooseberry	Parsnip	Honeysuckle	Cocoanut
Banana	Beetroot	Snowberry	Cones
Tomato	Marrow	Yew	Ash
Strawberry	Beans	Bryony	Maple
Plum	Etc.	Etc.	Honesty
Etc.			Etc.

62. General Plan of Lesson.—A carefully selected natural specimen is placed on a sheet of white paper to the left of the pupil, the drawing book or paper being immediately in front. When specimens are limited, as in the case of fruits, care must be taken that every pupil has a good view.

Several drawings may be made from the same object in different positions.

The teacher asks a few questions from a nature-study point of view in order to arouse interest. The structure of the object is elicited and the order in which it may be drawn; its special beauty is pointed out.

In most cases drawings are made slightly larger than the object, which will prevent actual measurements being transferred and does away with the temptation to trace or draw round the object.

During the lesson general faults are illustrated on the board and good points are mentioned. Individual assistance, by criticism chiefly, is of the highest importance.

In assessing the marks the artistic arrangement of the drawing on the paper, correctness of form, and expression of line will be considered. The pupils should be taught to use a soft line varying in thickness to show larger or smaller veins, etc.

Young pupils find much pleasure in using scissors to cut out their drawings, e.g. an ivy or laurel leaf may be cut out in green paper and mounted on a white sheet. This silhouetting of objects emphasises the form and helps the pupil to appreciate proportion.

63. Stages III. and IV.—More difficult natural objects, including the study of serrations and junctions of stalks, but without perspective.

Flowers.	*Leaves.*	*Fruits.*
Harebell	Virginia Creeper	*Groups of*—
Bluebell	Horse Chestnut	Cherries
Lily of Valley	Ivy ; Maple	Grapes
Wild rose	Nasturtium	Apples
Dahlia	Sycamore ; Walnut	Plums
Primrose	Plane ; Vine	Pears
Narcissus	Oak ; Geranium	Tomatoes
Daisy	Lupin ; Dandelion	Red Currants
Violet	Holly ; Elderberry	Medlars
Fuchsia	Jessamine	Damsons
Etc.	Chrysanthemum	Lemons
	Hawthorn ; Beech	Etc.
	Etc.	

Seeds and Berries.	*Sprays of Leaves.*	*Twigs and Small Boughs.*
Groups of—	Ivy	Horse Chestnut
Hawthorn	Virginia Creeper	Elm
Rose	Ash	Acacia
Whitebeam	Acacia	Plane
Cones	Jessamine	Ash
Elderberries	Rose	Lilac
	Willow	Beech
Ears of—	Blackberry	Bay
Wheat	Privet	Dogwood
Barley	Poplar	Holly
Oats	Hop	Hornbeam
Etc.	Etc.	Etc.

64. General Plan of Lesson.—As in First Stage; pupils should be taught to rely on their own observation and discover the plan of construction for themselves. The method of planning out and balancing masses before proceeding to details must be insisted on. A few specimen details such as serrations and junctions of stalks should be drawn by pupils and teacher to a larger scale. Fruits may be drawn in section as well as whole and in groups. Silhouetting may be carried out by painting the drawings with Indian ink or artists' black ; the veins of leaves and edges of overlapping petals, etc., are left white and the blacklead outline cleaned out, as in Fig. 29.

65. Stages V. and VI.—More advanced studies, including perspective and simple composition.

Flowers and buds.—

Wallflower	Dandelion	Anemone	Iris	Geranium
Stock	Buttercup	Nasturtium	Thistle	Rose
Jessamine	Sweet Pea	Narcissus	Orchid	Chicory
Convolvulus	Camellia	Daffodil	Cyclamen	Mallow, etc.

Sprays of Leaves and Flowers, including foreshortening. —Attention must be given to artistic selection and arrangement.

Ferns of various kinds.

Ribbonlike leaves, grasses, etc., involving study of twists (see Fig. 43).

Shells.—Oyster, mussel, snail, limpet, whelk, cockle, scallop, etc.

Feathers.—Fowl, parrot, wild duck, peacock, etc.

Outdoor sketching.—Methods of representing water, trees, clouds, etc. (see Art. 151).

66. General Plan of Lesson, as in other stages.—A flower-holder will be necessary, which should be placed as far from pupil as desk will allow. A small piece of clay or plasticine will answer the purpose. The form of flowers and sprays is shown to greater advantage if white paper is placed behind the specimen. Special attention should be given to the following points :—

The selection by the pupils of salient and characteristic features of the object.

The planning out and arranging of masses before inserting the details.

The accentuation of the line in finishing; the nearer edges to be represented by a bolder line.

The addition of light and shade and colour.

In outdoor sketching it is advisable to provide each pupil with a small sketch-book or several folds of drawing paper which can easily be held in one hand, but if seats are available a drawing board with paper and pins is most convenient. The outlines of hills and trees should first be attempted.

SOME PRINCIPLES OF BEAUTY, WITH METHOD OF
TEACHING.

67. Balance.—This is the most important principle in
the Arts. Exact symmetry is rarely found in Nature, but
balance is always present. Compare the balance of a leaf
on its midrib with the balance of the boughs of a tree.
Illustrate further by the balance of rhythm in music, the
balance of phrases in a sentence; a verse of poetry; a
statue; a building; and especially the balance in a good
picture.

Exercises.—*Simple Leaves, e.g.* laurel, lilac [Fig. 37
(*a*), (*b*)].

Draw midrib first; the curve of this will assist in
balancing the sides.

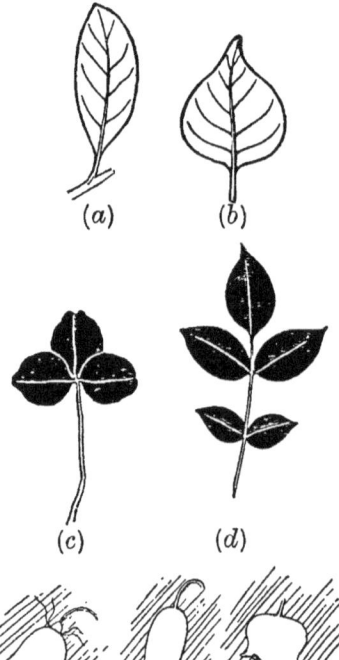

(*a*)   (*b*)

(*c*)   (*d*)

(*e*)   (*f*)   (*g*)

Fig. 37.

Compound Leaves, e.g. clo-
ver, rose [Fig. 37 (*c*), (*d*)].

Sketch centre line, midribs
of side leaves; notice angle
these make with stalk and
judge proportion of spaces;
draw leaves as before, omitting serrations.

*Simple Flowers, treated
flatly, e.g.* bluebell, harebell,
lily [Fig. 37 (*e*), (*f*), (*g*)].

Sketch and compare side
view of each; notice same
curve repeated in varying
proportion and see how curvature of stalk and pose of
flowers secure balance.

68. Radiation, *i.e.* the
convergence of lines to a
point. This is Nature's device to bring several objects
into one design and so secure
unity of effect.

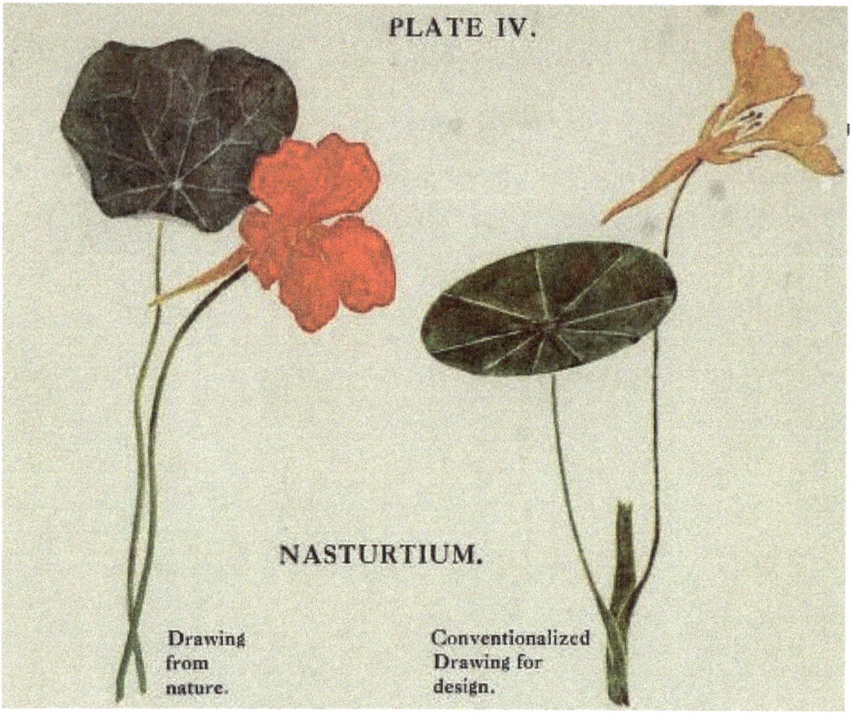

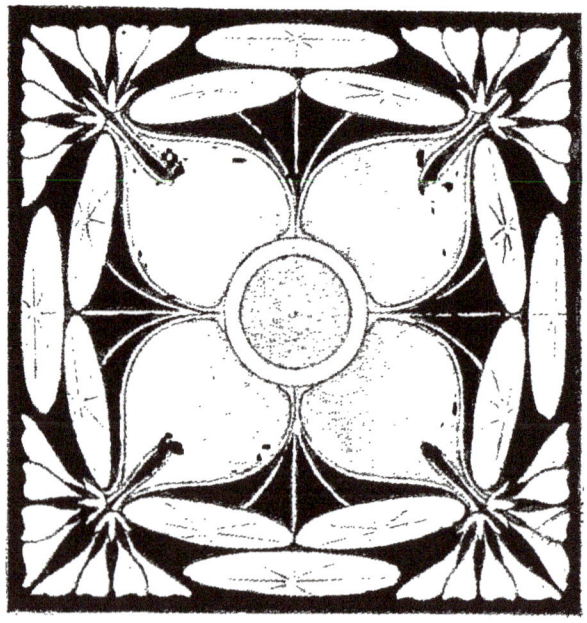

PLATE IV.

NASTURTIUM.

Drawing
from
nature.

Conventionalized
Drawing for
design.

Design for a Tile, based on the Nasturtium.

Exercises.—*Simple Leaves, e.g.* plantain, two kinds.

Compare proportions of the two specimens; each leaf has a principal vein; the radiation of the veins gives beauty.

Compound Leaves, e.g. ivy, Virginia creeper.

Notice that one leaf of the Virginia creeper is the chief or master leaf, two are slightly smaller, and two smaller still. This illustrates the Law of Principality and Subordination. Sketch chief veins; notice angles; balance each leaf.

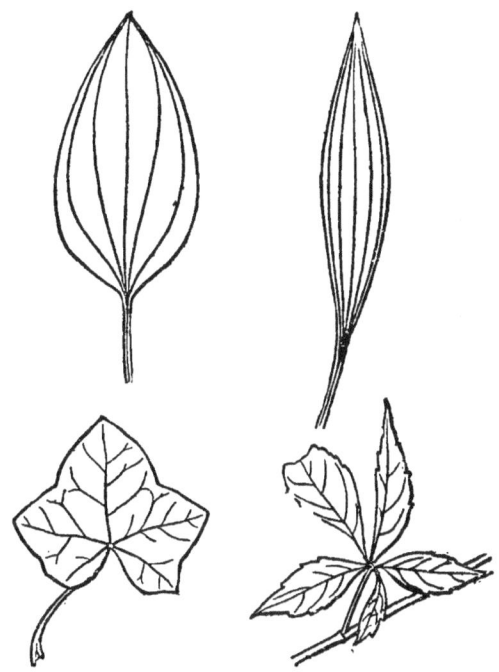

Fig. 38.

Shells, e.g. Limpet, Cockle.

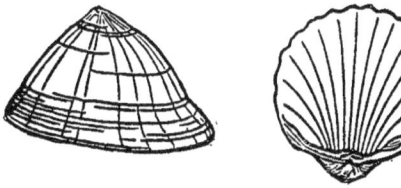

Fig. 39.

Flowers, e.g. daisy (full view), clematis.

Study shape of single petal; sketch outer circle by drawing two lines at right angles and make each quarter circle balance.

Petals of daisy may be drawn correct in number and position as follows:—Select one petal (mark it), draw this and opposite petal; draw and mark two nearest at right angles; the remaining petals should fit into their places.

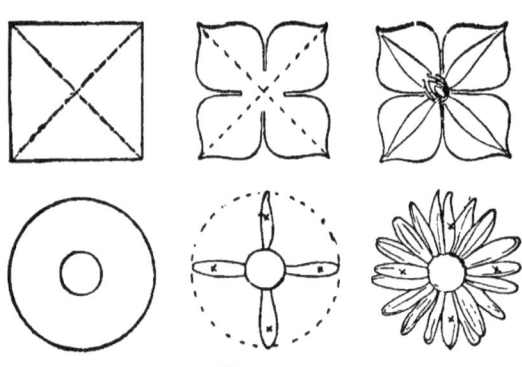

Fig. 40.

69. Repetition.—This is another of Nature's devices to secure unity of effect. The curves of the mountains, the shapes of the clouds, the forms of trees, rocks, flowers, and leaves all follow appointed laws. We must discover these laws and apply them to our drawings.

Exercises.—*Leaves, omitting serrations, e.g.* ash, acacia.

Compare shapes of leaves; study orderly arrangement; notice increase and decrease in size; examine junctions of stalks with main stem.

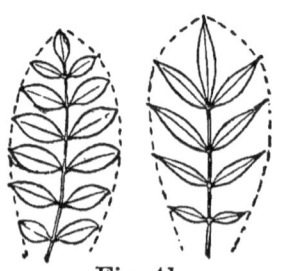

Fig. 41.

Leaves with serrations, e.g. sycamore (Fig. 42).

Follow stages as in illustration.

First Stage.—Draw the five leading veins and the general shape of the lobe round each.

Second Stage.—Each lobe is divided into three parts forming the larger serrations the curves of which correspond to the curves of the lobe itself. The secondary veins are inserted next.

Third Stage.—Each section is subdivided into three (there will be exceptions); the small serrations contain similar curves and are constructed in the same way as the larger ones. The smaller veins may now be drawn.

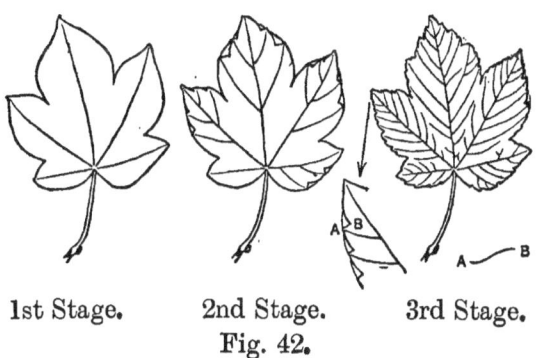

| 1st Stage. | 2nd Stage. | 3rd Stage. |

Fig. 42.

Illustrations of this Principle in Architecture, Music, and Literature should be given.

70. Curvature.—The most beautiful curves are the most difficult to draw. The beauty of bending and twisting leaves and petals is chiefly due to curvature.

Exercises.—*Ribbon-like Leaves,* e.g. variegated grass.

Large paper models will help. Plan out leading lines of leaves and stems as before. Study each twist carefully; draw hidden edge. Draw the same leaf in various positions (see Fig. 43).

Leaves without serrations, e.g. camellia leaf.

Practise drawing the leaf in all positions; in each case build and balance leaf on its chief vein (see Fig. 44).

Compare the curve of a melody, a well-turned sentence, gradation of light and shade and of colour.

71. Contrast.—Every beautiful object owes some of its beauty to this principle. We may observe in nature:—

Contrast of form, e.g. the elm tree: straight trunk of tree and rounded masses of foliage; the daffodil: circular flower and long narrow leaves ; the rose : smooth velvet petals and sharp thorns.

Contrast of colour, e.g. green foliage against a blue sky ; white daisies in the green grass ; red rose and green leaves.

Contrast in light and shade, e.g. the two sides of a stalk ; sunshine and shadow ; day and night.

Make use of this principle :—

In Outline Drawing.—Always draw the stalk in leaf and flower studies. The beauty of a flower is increased if its own leaves are added. In arranging flowers and sprays avoid formality and stiffness by placing one or two stalks in a different direction. A straight stalk crossing behind a flower or leaf will increase its beauty of form.

In Colouring.—Follow nature, *e.g.* green is a suitable contrast for any colour.

In Shading.—It will be found that a light leaf or petal is always next a darker one.

Note.—If the principles of beauty are taught from nature in this way, the pupils will be prepared to understand the laws of good ornament, they will know how to set about designing, and they may begin to study pictures of simple composition (see Art. 162). " *For though no one can invent by rule, there are some simple laws of arrangement which it is well for you to know, because, though they will not enable you to produce a good picture, they will often assist you to set forth what goodness may be in your work in a more telling way than you could have done otherwise ; and by tracing them in the work of good composers, you may better understand the grasp of their imagination, and the power it possesses over their materials.*"—RUSKIN.

It has been found that pupils in the higher classes are keenly interested in tracing these " laws of arrangement " in other school studies. They can see the artistic device of *contrast* in music, they recognise the principle of *repetition* in architecture and they can understand the *balance* of a good essay.

A Drawing of Variegated Grass, to illustrate the method
of drawing twisted leaves.

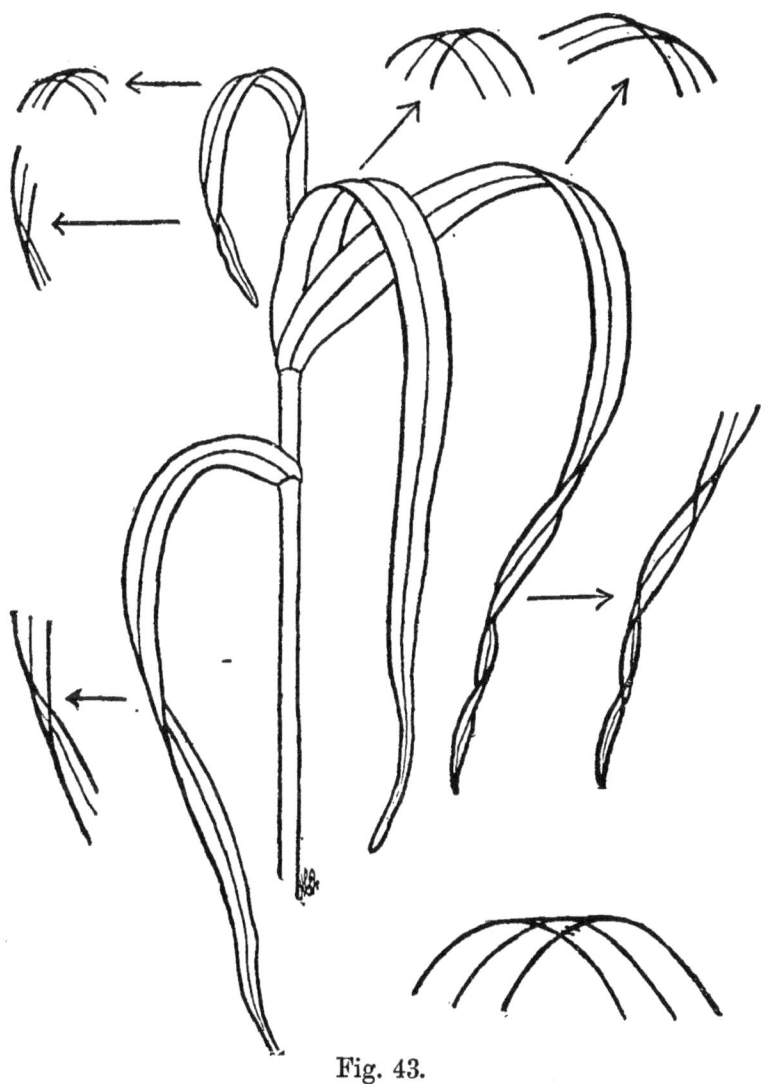

Fig. 43.

Drawings of a Camellia leaf in nine positions to illustrate
the beauty of *Curvature*.

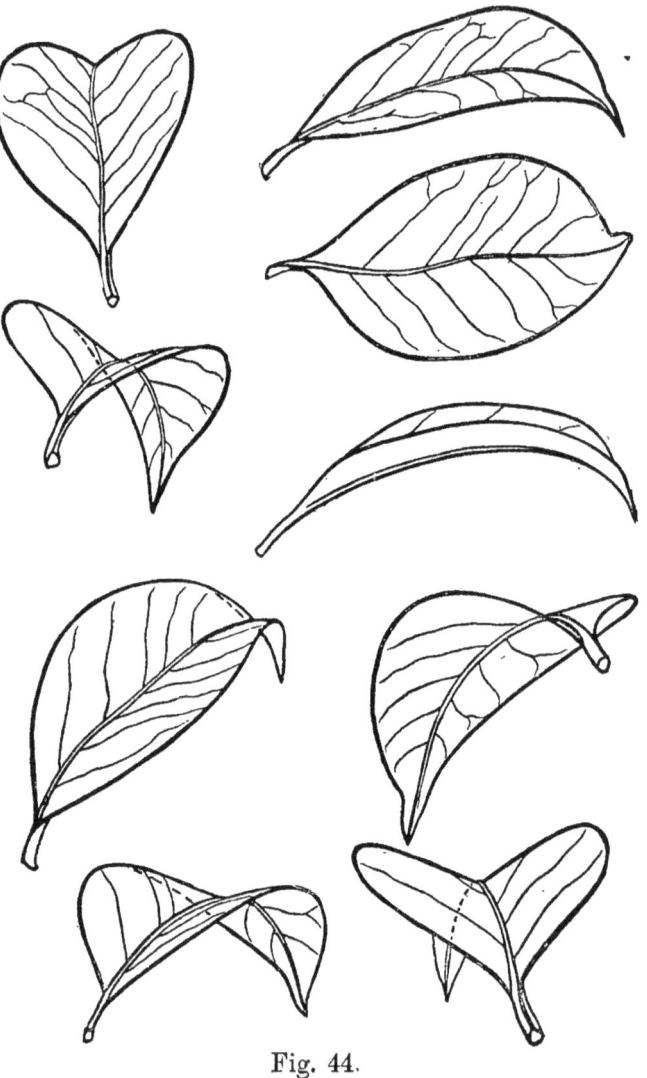

Fig. 44.

CHAPTER VI.

DRAWING FROM OBJECTS—WITHOUT PERSPECTIVE.

It is the natural progress of instruction to teach first what is obvious and perceptible to the senses, and from hence proceed gradually to notions large, liberal, and complete, such as comprise the more refined and higher excellencies in art.

SIR JOSHUA REYNOLDS.

72. The Value of Concrete Examples.—The advantage of the use of objects for drawing over that of "flat" copies has already been referred to.

The child obtains the necessary hand and eye training by pleasant means. His interest is maintained and his power of observation is exercised to the full. The "flat" copy, though of some educational value, should not be employed until a good foundation in drawing has been laid. This is a generally recognised principle in the teaching of other subjects, such as *Number*, where the concrete is dealt with before the abstract.

73. The disadvantages of a scheme of drawing based mainly on the use of objects are such as affect the teacher alone. Difficulties occur in the arrangement of a scheme, in the selection and procuring of suitable objects, and in displaying them in a proper manner. The earnest teacher, however, is not influenced by the ease or difficulty with which *his* share of the work is to be accomplished.

74. Points to be observed in the Selection of Objects for Drawing.

(1) The objects should be as *varied* as possible, all available sources, natural and artificial, to be laid under contribution.

(2) *Beauty of form* is an important consideration, and this will generally lead to the selection of a natural object in preference to an artificial one, where either will serve.

(3) The object must be chosen with the purpose of illustrating a *type form*. The indiscriminate use of *any* object or its selection merely on the score of novelty or showiness must be avoided. Its suitability, in all its details, must be considered carefully before the beginning of a lesson.

(4) A difficulty may be experienced sometimes in finding "pure" type forms in sufficient number, variety, or size. "Necessity" in this case should be "the mother of invention." Models may be made in clay or plasticine or cut out in paper or cardboard, tin, or thin wood.

(5) Objects in the class-room or about the school present a lack of variety and are soon exhausted. Calls should be made on household and personal belongings, especially of the children. A child takes a real interest in drawing a leaf or flower he himself has plucked, or a toy or tool, or small article he has brought from home.

Too much reliance, however, cannot be placed on this source of supply. A hint dropped by the teacher may result in the accumulation of a veritable heap of objects one day and *nothing* another time. Definite arrangements as to which children should bring the objects and instruction as to their exact form will be found necessary. In addition to this, a collection of suitable common objects should be kept in the school.

The character of the objects selected for drawing will be influenced largely by the locality of the school. Thus, in rural districts, natural forms, agricultural and gardening instruments, etc., will be more easily obtainable than in town schools.

75. Object Drawing Schemes.—Nature drawing is frequently taken as a subject distinct from and following artificial object drawing, just as the latter is sometimes made to follow the drawing of conventional forms from " the flat." Many natural forms offer less difficulty than drawing from objects or " the flat." Therefore, whatever classification of examples be made, the most logical method of selection will be according to—

(1) **The shape of the object,** whether a manufactured article or a natural form, such as a twig, leaf, bud, flower, fruit, shell, or insect.

(2) **The view presented**—thus, (*a*) *Flat*, showing two dimensions, length, and breadth, etc.; (*b*) *Solid*, showing three dimensions, length, breadth, and depth.

[Natural forms have been considered apart from artificial ones in this book as a matter of convenience, they should be used concurrently.]

An attempt has been made here at classification of objects according to their types. They are given merely in the way of suggestions, as it would be quite easy to select many more equally useful examples.

The order in which the type forms are taken need not necessarily be strictly adhered to, provided *some* logical order of work be adopted. Thus, practice in drawing *curved* forms may precede that of straight lines, and this is perhaps preferable in the case of freearm drawing.

76. Method of Displaying Objects for Drawing.— " Flat " objects to be drawn without perspective may be hung against the blackboard, or, better still, against a perfectly vertical surface, *e.g.* a wall or cupboard door. The object must be placed so that its surface is at right angles to the children's line of sight. For this purpose it may be necessary to set up several objects, one opposite each section of the class.

The object should be sufficiently large and placed at a height so that the children in the rear of the class can see it easily. Objects light in tone should be placed against a dark background, and dark objects should be placed against a light background.

Where the object is small, such as a reel, a specimen should be provided for every two scholars at least.

Solid objects, to be drawn in elevation, may be placed on or slightly above the children's eye-level on the teacher's table or on a shelf, window-sill, etc., or suspended by a string fastened to a nail, or attached to a line stretched across the room.

The following exercises may be executed in any style, outline or mass, in chalk, crayon, pencil, or brush.

STAGE I.

77. Easy Straight-lined Forms.—*Horizontal, vertical, and oblique lines:* Sticks of various lengths, strips of coloured paper, lead-pencils, pen and crayon holders, matches, etc., drawn singly or in groups, or placed to form the following:—

Right-angled forms.—Capital letters, L, H, T, F, E.

A wooden sword—made of laths placed at various angles (see Fig. 45).

[NOTE: The difficulty of these exercises is greatly increased when the objects are placed obliquely.]

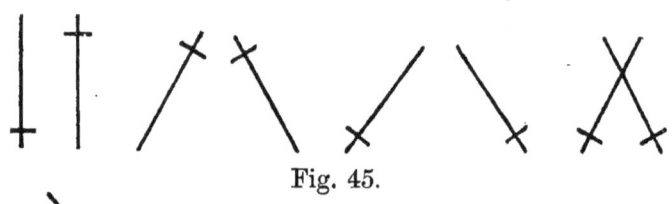

Fig. 45.

Simple rectangular forms.—Blackboard, book-covers of various proportions, ruler, tram-tickets, bricks, brickwork.

Post-cards, envelopes (front view) of various shapes and in different positions.

Rectangular solids in elevation; matchbox, pencil and chalk boxes. Windows, panes, and sills.

Rectangular face of parcel tied with string.

Stage II.

78. More Difficult Rectangular Forms, the Triangle and other Straight-lined Figures.

Capital letters, V, A, N, Z, Y, M, W.
2-foot rule opened at different angles.
Numerals, 7, 4.
Square and oblong sheets of paper, corners folded back.
Paper folded to produce hat, boat (Figs. 46, 47, 48).

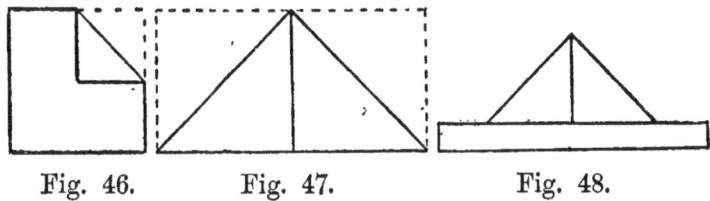

Fig. 46.   Fig. 47.   Fig. 48.

Envelopes—back views; flaps open. Also, front view with address and stamp.
Set squares in different positions.
Musical triangle.
Book-cover or portfolio, with rectangular label and leather corners.
Picture-frame and cord, garden spade.

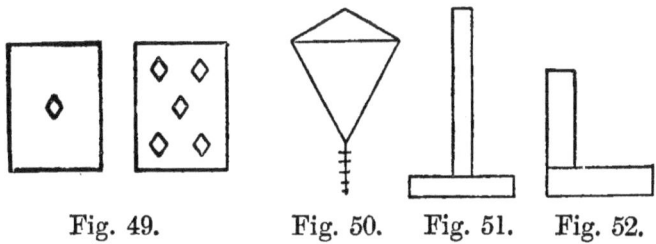

Fig. 49.   Fig. 50.   Fig. 51.   Fig. 52.

Diamond shape.—Playing cards, toy kite (Figs. 49, 50).
Luggage labels, back and front view.
T-square, try-square (Figs. 51 and 52). Large hinge (Fig. 53).

Block letters—straight-line capitals cut out of paper or cardboard (Fig. 54).

Flags various, St. George, St. Andrew, etc.   Union Jack.

Banners attached to pole (Fig. 55).

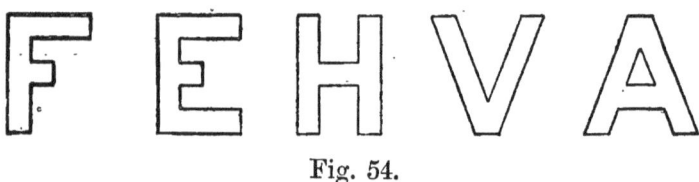

Fig. 54.

Teacher's desk in elevation, school easel, straight-lined toy-house, Noah's ark, etc., school satchel and strap, maltese cross.

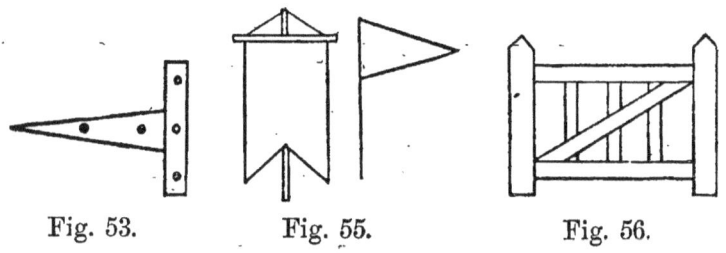

Fig. 53.   Fig. 55.   Fig. 56.

Pictures of simple objects, cut-out in card or paper, such as a house or gate (Fig. 56).

Simple round forms—of straight line elevation—drum, jar, straw hat, flower-pot, mallet, etc. (Figs. 57-60).

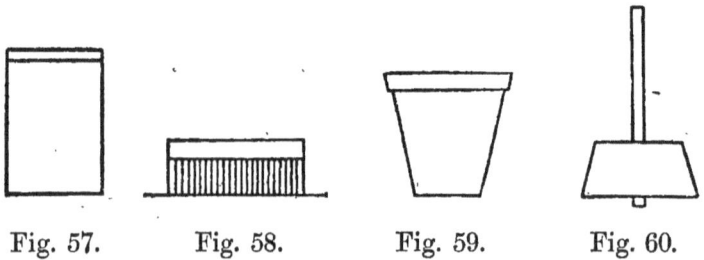

Fig. 57.   Fig. 58.   Fig. 59.   Fig. 60.

Pattern-laying and Drawing, leading to *Elementary Design.* By way of additional practice in straight line drawing, freehand, freearm, or ruler, on plain or squared paper, simple repeating patterns may be constructed (and afterwards drawn) by the children, by means of short sticks or coloured strips of cardboard, tablets, or shapes— (see Figs. 61-68).

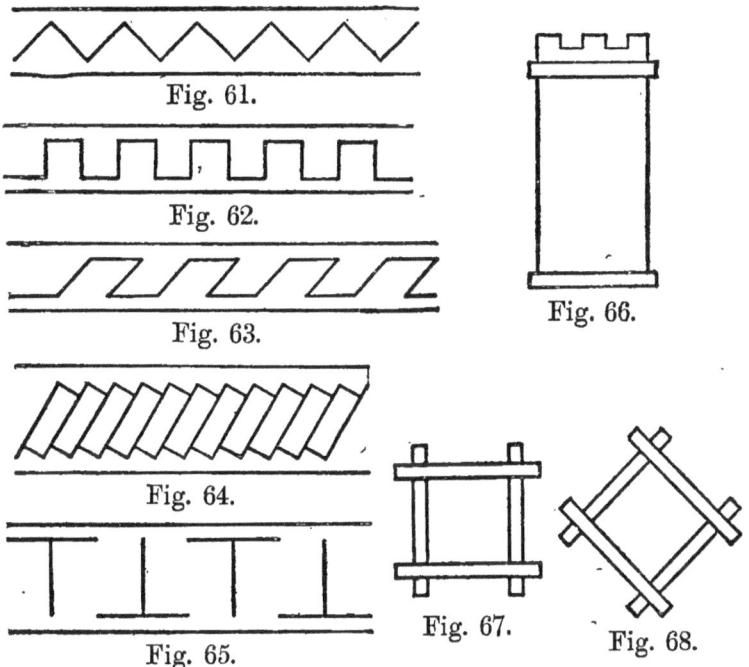

Fig. 61.

Fig. 62.

Fig. 63.

Fig. 64.

Fig. 65.

Fig. 66.

Fig. 67.

Fig. 68.

STAGE III.

79. Curved Forms.

The Circle.—The number of purely circular forms is limited and the drawing of them alone is apt to become monotonous. *Examples:* Hoops, coins, watch, clock, wheels, biscuits.

Spherical forms.—A ball; the same suspended from a string; marbles, hat-pins.

STAGE IV.

80. Simple Curves and Straight Lines Combined.— (Natural forms, such as cherries, orange, currants, might be introduced at this stage).

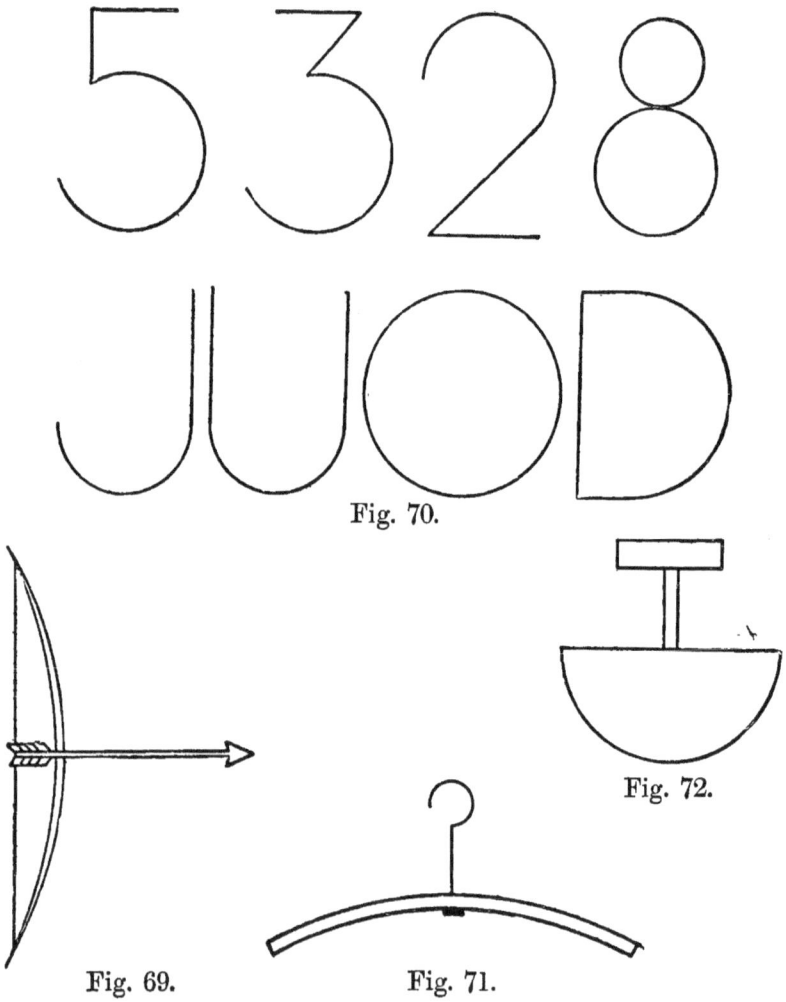

Fig. 70.

Fig. 72.

Fig. 69.   Fig. 71.

A large bow and arrow, placed in various positions. This is a most useful example; the curves can be varied by tightening the cord and the depth estimated by the aid of the arrow placed at right angles to it (Fig. 69).

Letters and numerals based on circular and other curves (Fig. 70): these, as well as shield and other forms, may be cut out of white paper in duplicate and to a large scale.

Curved-handled walking-stick, hockey stick, whip, hairpins, coat-hanger (Fig. 71), wire-hooked letter file, banjo.

Semi-circular forms.—Cheese-cutter (Fig. 72), tobacco-pouch, paper kite.

STAGE V.

81. More Advanced Curves—including the ellipse, oval and cordate or heart-shaped forms.

These curves should be taken in the above order. In the Practice stage, cut-out forms as described (Art. 39) should be freely used.

Natural forms, such as fruits (gooseberry, peach, plum), potato; seed and bud forms; eggs, etc., should be introduced.

Artificial Objects.—Football, threaded beads (circular and elliptical), photo-frame (elliptical or circular opening), rush-fan, knife-board, tailor's pressing-board, meat-hook (**S**-shaped), horse-shoe, horse-shoe magnet, stirrup, toy spade (wooden), wooden spoon, cricket bat, padlock, bootjack.

In simple elevation: Salt-grater; hard and soft felt and silk hats; large shovel, gridiron, wire toasting-fork; large keys; bicycle hand and foot pumps, rolling-pin, towel roller, candle, stencil brush, bulrush, pestle, flat gum-brush, long-handled broom, yard broom.

STAGE VI.

82. Objects. Introducing Compound Curves.

Examples: Table spoon, hand-mirror, hand-brush, tennis racket, hand-bellows, Japanese fans; table-knife, pocket-knife (blades shut or open at different angles), fork, eye-glasses, spectacles.

Garden implements: Fork, shovel, etc.

Farming implements: Reaping hook, scythe, etc.

STAGE VII.

83. Vases.—[Concurrently with this stage the perspective of the circle in a horizontal position might be conveniently taken. Thus the following examples can be made to serve a double purpose—they may be drawn (1) in elevation, (2) in perspective.

Vase forms in elevation (*i.e.* lines which are circular in plan are represented by horizontal straight lines).

Vases present varied and subtle forms. Extreme care must be taken in judging (1) Proportions of the different parts, neck, body, foot, etc.—these must be set off along the centre line—and of the varying widths. (2) The *exact* shape of the profiles. A great aid will be found in the use of backgrounds of contrasting tone, and in mass drawing or demonstration by means of cut-out paper.

Bottle shapes.—Water bottle, wine bottles, long and short-necked, spirit and mineral water bottles (stone and glass, cork and screw-stoppered), beer or ink jars, cream jars, Indian club, skittle, opera glasses, bulb glasses, lamp chimneys and shades, gas globes, gold-fish globe (with water, and suspended by string), wine glasses, egg-cup and egg.

Hand-bell, gramaphone horn.

STAGE VIII.

84. Advanced forms—in elevation. Tobacco pipes—of difficult shape, toy boats, knife and roller skates, boots, shoes, etc.

Musical instruments : Bugle, cornet, violin, mandoline.

Carpenter's tools and other implements—hand-saw, tenon-saw, bow-saw, gimlet, stock and bit, callipers, pincers, scissors, tongs, air-gun, pistol, sword.

CHAPTER VII.

DRAWING OF OBJECTS IN PERSPECTIVE.

A student is not always advancing because he is employed;
he must apply his strength to that part of the art where the
real difficulties lie.—SIR JOSHUA REYNOLDS.

85. Use of the Geometrical Models.—It is now
generally recognised that practice in drawing from the
geometrical models and common objects should not be
separated. Owing to their misuse the geometrical models
have fallen somewhat into discredit, and in some instances
have been abolished.

The ultimate aim is to draw surrounding objects of
average difficulty. The type models, on account of their
simplicity of form, are a very useful means of attaining
that aim. Their use, however, should be discontinued
when the principles they are intended to illustrate have
been made clear. The most useful type models are the
cylinder, cone, cube and square prism.

The system by which the children are "taught" to draw
each of the models in turn in set positions, usually commencing with the cube, cannot be too strongly condemned.
After many illustrations, hints and rules on the part of the
teacher and much tedious practice, the child may produce a
tolerably accurate drawing of the model when placed in a
particular position. The drawing is produced, probably, by
an effort of memory rather than of judgment, much in the
same way as a child will sometimes "read off" a page of
a book with which he is familiar—after *spelling* the first
word.

86. Seating Arrangements.—A difficulty in connection with object drawing is the matter of seating so that each child may get an uninterrupted view of the object. This difficulty does not arise where the object is placed above the scholars' eye-level.

The ideal condition for conducting the lesson is a room with ample floor-space, so that the seats may be ranged round the object easily in the form of a circle, semicircle,. or horse-shoe. The desks must be placed at right angles to imaginary lines radiating from the centre of the object or group. Otherwise, the children must be thoroughly drilled into turning directly towards the object for the purposes of observation, if it be impossible to do so while drawing. Neglect of this rule may lead to a great deal of faulty drawing, especially in the estimation of the direction of straight lines.

In the ordinary class-room a clear space in front of the desks is essential. If the floor is not " stepped " the desks may be turned so as to face the object directly.

Should this arrangement be impracticable, the class should be divided into two or three sections, each taking a practice lesson in turn, while the remainder takes some other form of drawing, or duplication of the object may meet the difficulty. Demonstration lessons may be given to the class as a whole.

87. Position of the Object.—Although a distance of about eighteen inches above the ground is usually best, the height of the object should be varied frequently. Children who have been trained to draw objects at a fixed level are often hopelessly at sea when the object is placed *above* the eye-level, lines which should converge downwards are drawn upwards, and circular forms especially are represented as though below the eye-level.

Large objects should be used when studying a new type or principle. At a later stage small objects, *e.g.* a cotton reel, ink-well, match-box, etc., may be employed, not more than two children working from the same object if dual desks are used. The object should then be placed on the desk in *front* of the one from which it is to be drawn.

88. The First Principle of Perspective Projection. —The movements described as Imaginary Drawing (Art. 32) must be applied again; the outline should be traced in the air at arm's length. When representing solidity or depth the children must be impressed continually with the idea that a tracing is to be made on a vertical wall or sheet of glass set up at right angles to their line of sight, between them and the object. (The term Picture Plane, which this represents, need not be mentioned.) At this stage there is a continual mental conflict between the knowledge of the actual form of an object and its particular appearance.

89. Experimental Use of the Picture Plane.—In order to gain the children's interest and convince them that "things are not what they seem," drawings should be made on a vertical glass plane. A fairly large window-pane will serve the purpose. The teacher should stand well back from the glass, keep perfectly steady, and with the left eye closed (the necessity for this should be explained; a left-handed person would need to close the *right* eye) the main lines of the opposite building may be traced with a piece of pointed soap, damp chalk, or brush and thick whitewash. A simple object, such as a box or flower-pot, might be mounted on the window-sill outside and similarly traced. Some practice is required in order to gain the necessary steadiness of hand and eye.

The children should be encouraged to make these "pictures" for themselves at home and submit freehand copies of the tracings to the teacher. All the principles of perspective may be demonstrated in this way. The model of the Picture Plane might be employed whenever a fresh difficulty is introduced.

90. Advantages of Commencing with Circular Forms.—A great difficulty in dealing with large classes is that many of the principles have to be brought home to the children more or less individually. They must be convinced by *seeing for themselves*. It is well to limit the number of views possible at a time, hence the advantage of dealing with *upright* cylindrical forms first. Unlike the rectangular solids, their appearance is not materially altered nor the drawing complicated by varying the position of the spectator.

Another advantage is that a vast range of interesting objects suitable for drawing is opened up, when once the representation of the circle in a horizontal position has been mastered.

Demonstration and short training exercises in the judgment of the apparent depth of receding rectangular surfaces may be taken concurrently with the drawing of round forms preparatory to the next stage.

91. Experiment 1: Demonstrating the Fore-shortening of Horizontal Circular Surfaces.—Mark off and figure boldly a number of equal divisions (say, one

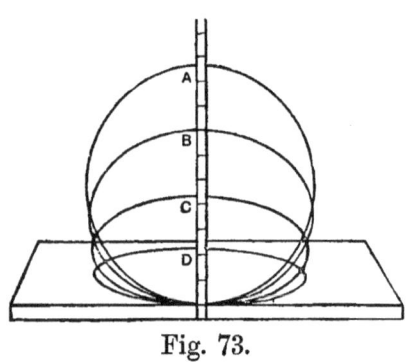

Fig. 73.

inch apart) along a long lath or straight-edge. Fix this upright or screw into the edge of a drawing-board or stand placed below the level of the children's eyes (Fig. 73). Place a hoop or cardboard disc vertically against the lath (Position A), so that its surface is at right angles to the children's line of sight. [*Note.*—The children should be ranged in files, not more than two or three abreast, the eye-levels rising towards the rear, so that each child gets an uninterrupted view of the model. It may be necessary to repeat the experiment to the class in sections.]

The length of the vertical diameter of the circle is shown by means of the lath and will appear alike to all. The hoop should be turned back slowly until it rests horizontally on the board (Position D). The movement should be arrested at intervals, the children being required to state the apparent depth of the curve as indicated by the vertical lath. One eye must be kept closed during this operation, otherwise a stereoscopic view will be obtained and the necessary impression of the curve intersecting the line of the lath at a particular height will be lost. The apparent depth will vary according to the height of the child's eye. The fact that the major diameter of the curve remains fairly constant must be insisted upon throughout the experiment.

92. Experiment 2 : Use of the Gauge for any Horizontal Surface.—This apparatus will be of great value also where difficulty is experienced in estimating the apparent depth of *any* horizontal surface. Suppose it be required to gauge the comparative horizontal depth of the drawing board, the distance of its front edge from the face of the cube, and the depth of the top surface of the cube. The lath should be fixed as shown in the diagram (Fig. 74), and

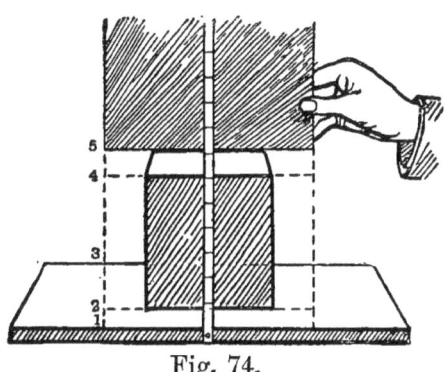

Fig. 74.

a rectangular sheet of cardboard set up against it so as to obscure the model, the lower edge resting at 1. The " shutter " is then raised slowly, each child notifying the teacher by raising its hand when the several horizontal edges come into view—at 1, 2, 3, 4, 5 (Fig. 74). These distances will be shown on the gauge, and of course will vary according to the height of eye.

93. Experiment 3, and 1st Practice.—The apparatus (Fig. 75) consists of two upright rods with small blocks attached and fixed into a bottom board. By resting a disc on these at varying heights and keeping its surface perfectly horizontal its apparent diminution of depth may be demonstrated, until the eye-level is reached, when it appears as a horizontal line. It should then be moved *above* the eye-level, when it will be observed that the nearest point in the curve appears higher than the farthest, the surface having an apparently downward direction.

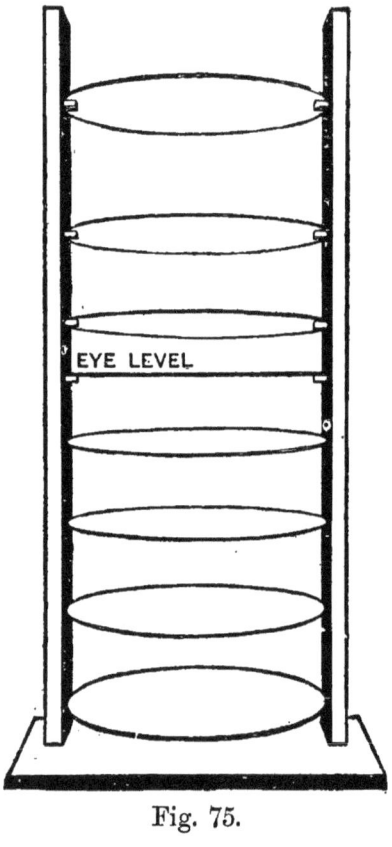

EYE LEVEL

Fig. 75.

This apparatus may be used in the same manner with square, triangular, or other shaped planes. The fact that a horizontal plane of any shape in the eye-level appears as a straight line may be demonstrated easily in this way.

94. Other Apparatus for Estimating the Apparent Depth of Receding Plane Surfaces.—The following device will be found useful. A large sheet of cardboard has a circular, square, or triangular opening made so that the portion cut out may be revolved on an axis or pin. If the four edges of the board are bent back as shown in the diagram (Fig. 76), the model will stand upright so that the axis of the cut-out portion is either horizontal as a and b or vertical as c and d. The planes may be revolved so as to present any degree of foreshortening required.

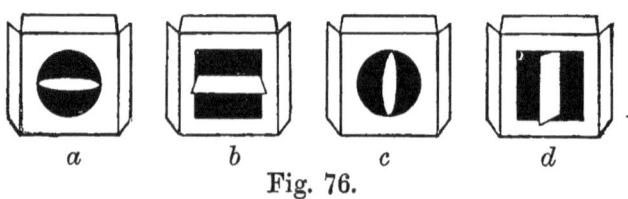

a   b   c   d
Fig. 76.

The appearance and depth of the plane may be readily estimated by comparing it with the height and width of the aperture, which it fits exactly. Smaller models, for individual practice, may be made by the children.

95. Drawing of Cylindrical Forms.—The geometrical model in an upright position may be taken as a first exercise. The following are some common errors in the drawing of the cylinder :—

1. The ellipses drawn as *a* and *b* (Fig. 77). (See Art. 42 for the proper method of drawing the ellipse.)

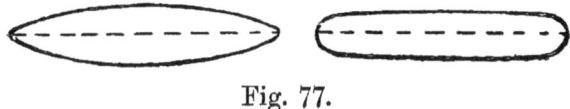

Fig. 77.

2. Proportionate depth of upper and lower ends neglected or wrongly estimated.

3. Curve of the lower end not represented tangential to the sides of the cylinder (see Fig. 78). This is due to the visible portion only of the base being drawn. The drawing of the *whole* of such curves in the preliminary sketch should be insisted on. (This applies also to the drawing of the cone.)

Cylindrical Objects. — Boxes, canisters of various proportions such as preserved meat, milk, fruit tins ; jam or pickle jars (with or without labels), incandescent gas mantle box, round china palette, coins (singly and in piles), drum, men's linen collars, sieve, scroll of paper, squirt or glass syringe, candle, tub, barrel, peaked cap, straw

Fig. 78.

and other hats, wood or iron dumbbell. *Objects from the school laboratory*, *e.g.* beakers, flasks, circular water-trough, etc. (For further examples see curved forms, Chap. VI., Stages VI. and VII.)

96. The Cone (vertical position).—A cardboard disc with a rod attached upright at its centre—to represent the base and axis of a cone—should be drawn first. A vertical axis, which is represented as a continuation of the minor diameter of the base, must always be employed so that the apex of the cone shall be represented exactly vertically over the centre of the base. Care must be taken that the "sides" of the cone are drawn tangential to the curve of the base.

A model of the disc and rod inverted will prove a useful exercise for drawing, and suggests a Chinese parasol, which may be attempted next.

97. The Truncated Cone.—Two unequal discs pierced centrally and at right angles by a rod are the basis of this model. It should be drawn in two positions, the larger and then the smaller disc being the base in turn. In completing the representation of the truncated cone, care must be taken to draw the straight lines of the "sides" tangential to the ends.

Further Examples.—A *cone* with a number of circles boldly marked parallel to the base, glass tumbler, flowerpot, funnel, china or glass (unspillable) ink-well, sugar basin, cardboard lamp-shades, incandescent electric-light shade and burner (above the eye-level), Chinese umbrella (partly open), lubricating oil-can, shuttlecock, shaving brush, boy's Eton collar (see also Chap. VI., Curved Forms, Stages VI. and VII.), kaleidoscope, milk churn.

98. The Sphere.—A large ball or the school globe will represent this.

The Hemisphere and Dome-shaped Forms are useful and common types.

A large sphere with two or three parallel bands painted or boldly marked on its surface will provide a number of useful exercises ; thus :—

(1) The sphere suspended below the eye-level, the rings being horizontal.

(2) The same suspended *above* the eye-level.

(3) Representation of portions of the sphere cut by a horizontal plane at a point indicated at any given distance from the top or bottom of the sphere when suspended above or below the eye-level. Upper, lower, or middle portions should be represented.

These forms are the bases of objects such as: bowls, basins, saucers (also inverted) of various descriptions, gold-fish bowl, half-orange, apple, turnip, etc.; mushroom; buns, table-bell, helmets, hats and caps, open umbrella, toy cup and ball, Chinese lanterns (various profiles), and more advanced forms such as hanging, table, and reading lamps. (See also Chap. VII., Curved Forms, Stages VI. and VII.)

The *School globe* may be drawn at this stage with its axis in a vertical position, showing the lines of the equator and the zones.

Miscellaneous Objects seen out-of-doors.—(Suitable for memory drawing.) Chimney-pots and cowls, pillar-box, electric-light lamp and standard.

CHAPTER VIII.

PERSPECTIVE REPRESENTATION OF STRAIGHT-LINED OBJECTS.

Drawing is an obvious convention, for we do not see lines round or upon an object but one tint adjusted against another. Yet it comes more naturally to us to represent things by this convention of lines than by tones and gradations.—G. CLAUSEN, R.A.

99. Estimation of Depth of Receding Surfaces.— Prepare a number of pieces of tape (two bright colours), each about a foot long, with some small object, such as a leaden pellet, attached to the end of each. Stretch a line taut across the class-room, facing the class. From this line and opposite each section of the class suspend two pieces of tape of the same colour about a foot apart. Let the children draw these in the air, and then on their paper or boards, noting the proportion between their length and distance apart.

Next, stretch a second cord across the room at the same height and parallel to and about 1 foot behind the first. Immediately behind each of the first suspended tapes hang another of the same length and contrasting colour. The children should trace these lines in the air, estimating the apparent distance to the right or left of the front ones and draw them. Accuracy of length of these lines need not be insisted upon at this stage. The difference between the actual and apparent distances between the front and rear vertical lines should then be discussed.

100. " Drill " Preparatory to Measurement at Sight.—Though not usually associated with the teaching of Drawing, some form of "drill" is necessary where it is required to direct the movements of a *class*. The following movements should be practised, therefore, again and again, the children carrying them out simultaneously at word of command.

Position 1.—The pencil is held horizontally by pressing the extremities between the tip of the first finger of each hand (see Fig. 79). It is then brought backward to the

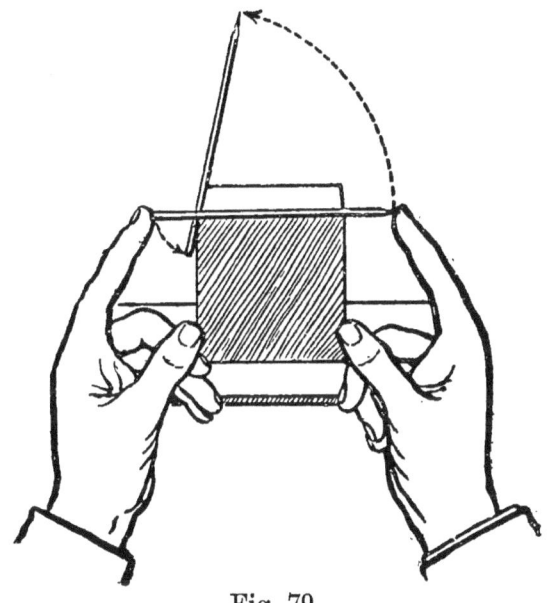

Fig. 79.

level of the eyes and with a smart movement thrust forward, so as to be perfectly parallel with the line of the shoulders and the long edge of the desk. The left eye must be kept closed.

Position 2.—Remove all the hanging tapes except those opposite the centre section of the class. These will represent the four vertical edges of a pendant cube. The children should hold their pencils at arm's length, as described (Position 1), and on the word of command turn in their seats so as to face the model directly; the arms should be kept perfectly rigid while the body is turned. By moving the pencil vertically up and down, each child will describe his picture plane (at right angles to his line of sight). It is in such a vertical plane that *all distances* are to be estimated in future.

Practice.—Each child should now estimate the relative positions of the vertical tapes from his point of view, and then draw them, always commencing with the nearest or "prime vertical."

Similar practice may be obtained by setting up skittles or rods (the latter may be stuck in clay or plasticine) on the teacher's table, so that they may be seen by the whole class.

101. Measurement at Sight.—The children should be trained to rely upon the judgment of the eye for proportionate measurements. When this fails, the pencil

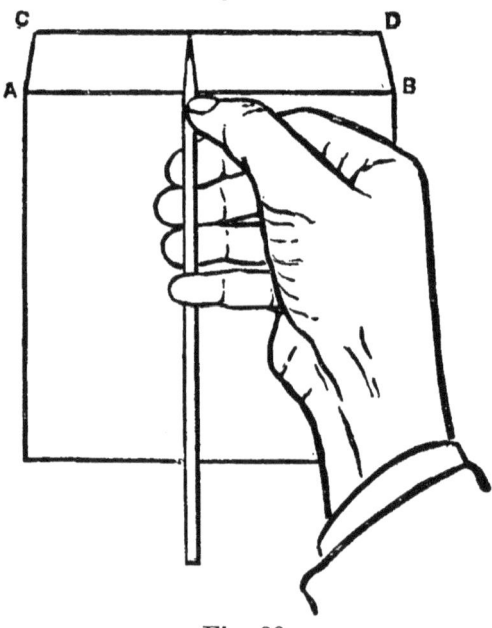

Fig. 80.

may be held at arm's length, the left eye being closed, and moved rapidly across the imaginary picture plane so as to cover the angles or edges of objects. The relative distances will be thus visualised.

As a further *means of verification* the following method may be adopted :—Hold the pencil vertically at arm's length, the ball of the thumb and little finger nail being pressed against the near side of the pencil and the tips of the other three fingers on the outside, so that the thumb-nail can be moved freely along the pencil, which can be turned at the same time at any angle with the ground, while always remaining parallel to the picture plane. (See Fig. 80.)

No actual measurements are to be made in this way. It is merely a means of establishing a proportion between distances. Thus, if it be required to measure the apparent depth of the top surface of the cube (Fig. 80), the pencil is held as described above, so that one end covers a point in the edge CD. The thumb-nail acts as a gauge, and is moved down the pencil until it coincides with a point in the nearer edge AB. This distance is then moved verti-cally *in the same imaginary plane* and measured into the height of the front face of the cube. The pencil thus serves the purpose of the lath in the apparatus described (Art. 92). With a quick move-ment of the wrist the depth of the top face may be divided into the edge AB.

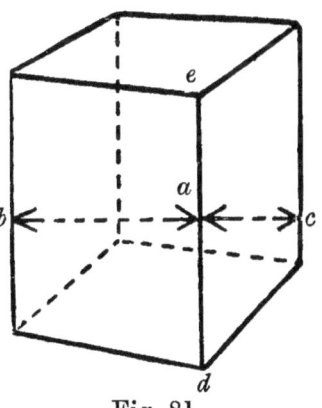

It is frequently necessary to compare horizontal distances with other horizontal or vertical dis-tances (thus *ab* with *ac* or *de*, Fig. 81).

Lines which recede at *any* angle from the ground or the picture plane may also be measured in this way, providing that in turning the wrist the pencil is kept strictly parallel to the picture plane.

Fig. 81.

102. Representation of Straight Lines which Recede.—This is the most difficult point for beginners. Mere lecturing on principles of perspective, such as the convergence of parallel lines which recede, even when accompanied by elaborate blackboard sketches, is of little value. Children as a rule readily admit the truth of things they are expected to see. Recourse should be had to some simple device, such as the transparent plane (see Art. 89), that will enable children to arrive at truths for themselves. The knowledge thus gained may be embodied in the form of rules for subsequent application.

The study of photographic views or pictures (suitable illustrations may be found in the school reading books) will prove interesting to children when they have obtained some knowledge of perspective in order to demonstrate the manner in which the principles have been applied.

103. Experiment for Gauging the Apparent Direction of Receding Lines.—It is usual to begin by drawing

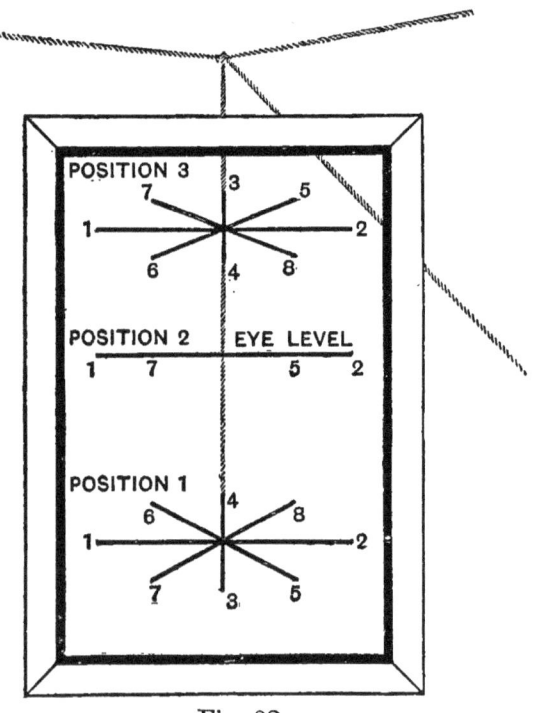

Fig. 82.

the cube or large drawing board in a horizontal position. For demonstration purposes, however, the following simple model will be found useful (Fig. 82). Suspend a long lath by means of a cord attached to the middle so that it lies parallel to the ground, about 2 feet below the children's eye-level. It is an advantage if the object can be drawn up to any level above or below the eye. The class should be supplied with rulers or lead pencils and ranged round the model.

A fairly large sheet of glass, framed if possible, may be used in place of the usual model of the picture plane, if this be not available. This should be held perfectly upright, say, by two of the scholars in front of each of the scholars in turn at a distance of his arm's length, at right angles to his line of sight and between him and the suspended lath. The pencil or ruler should be held as described (Art. 100, *Position* 1) and pressed firmly and revolved against the glass plane by each child, the cord and lath being thus "covered" in turn by raising or depressing either hand. The head must be kept steady and the left eye closed.

104. Facts Learnt from Observation.—It should be explained that in drawing the paper or board takes the place of this sheet of glass, which may be imagined to be set up thus always. Individual scholars may be called upon in turn to draw the lines of the model on the blackboard as seen from their point of view, when the following facts should be elicited :—

(1) Vertical lines (such as that of the cord) are always represented thus.

(2) Horizontal lines (that is, those parallel to the ground) may assume *any* direction on the picture plane, as 1–2, 5–6, or even vertical, as 3–4. (Position 1, Fig. 82.)

(3) Lines that are parallel to the picture plane are drawn in their true direction.

(*Note :* This is a universal rule, Rule 1 being a particular case. It also applies to lines inclined to the ground.)

The lath may then be raised *in the eye-level*. (Position 2.) It will be represented by a horizontal line, whatever direction it assumes with the glass plane, varying from the full length to a single point, according to its direction.

When raised *above* the eye-level, the line appears to take a *downward* direction, the farther extremity appearing *lower* than the near one. (Position 3.)

105. 2nd Practice in Gauging the Direction of Receding Lines.—Arrange the class round a large cube or a rectangular horizontal surface situated below the eye-level, such as a drawing-board or top of teacher's table. At the word of command let the children cover the nearer adjacent edges of the objects in turn with their lead pencils without the aid of the glass plane, in the manner already described. The "covering" movement for each line should

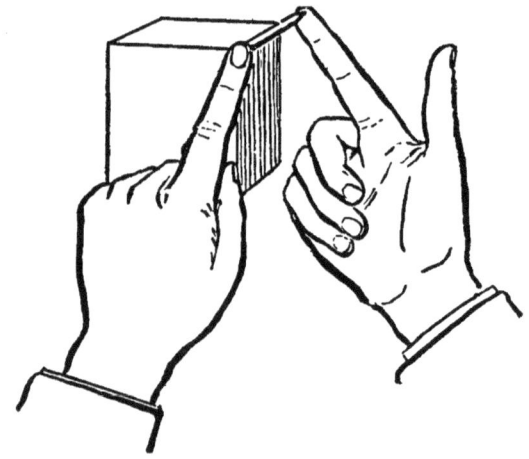

Fig. 83.

be repeated several times, *both* eyes being opened at the end of the operation to note the direction the pencil assumes with a horizontal base line. Where the line recedes somewhat directly from the spectator and its apparent direction approaches the vertical the pencil may be held upright first and the angle made with it carefully observed.

There is a tendency at first to stretch one hand further forward than the other, making the pencil point in the direction in which the edge of the object recedes, as is shown in Fig. 83. The extremities of the pencil should be moved directly *upward or downward* like those of the beam of a balance. Figs. 79 and 84 show the correct movements.

The advantages of this form of drill are that the teacher can tell at a glance whether the children can estimate the

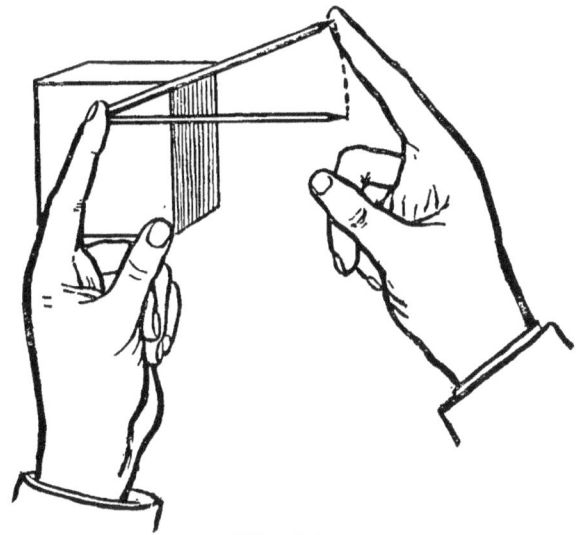

Fig. 84.

apparent direction of a receding line correctly; each child knows exactly what is required of him when set to draw, and will have a ready means, in the earlier stages at least, of verifying or rectifying his work.

106. Lines Inclined to the Ground.—The method described of gauging the apparent direction of receding horizontal lines may be applied to straight lines in *any* direction. Thus, if the cord attached to the lath (Fig. 82) be slipped nearer one end, the lath will become inclined to the ground, and in this position is usually difficult to represent. Where the eye has been trained to seek a " covering " line this difficulty disappears. Fig. 85 is the representation of a portion of a writing-desk when the eye is opposite the extreme left of the object. The sloping, horizontal, and vertical edges on the left are all obscured by the side of the pencil held upright, while the corresponding edges on the right are represented in different directions.

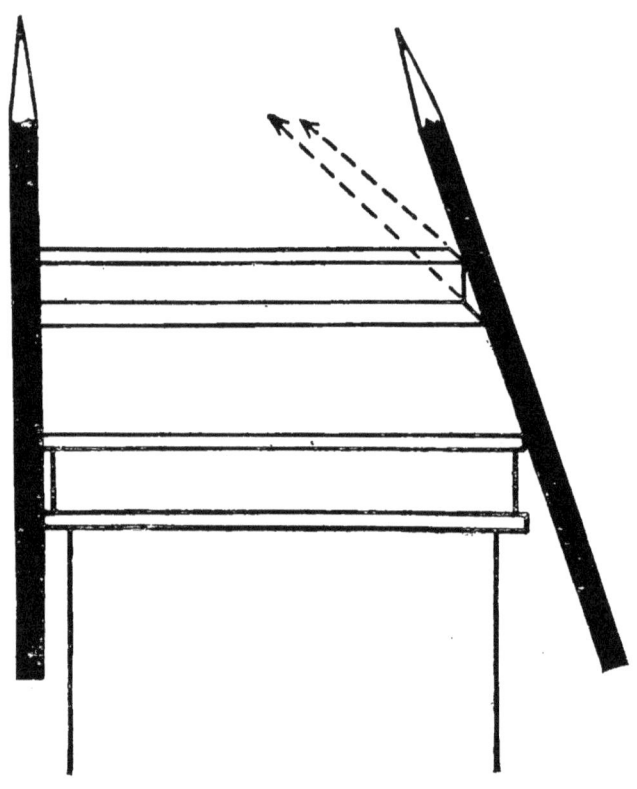

Fig. 85.

107. Convergence of Parallel Lines which Recede. —The children must be led to observe this phenomenon for themselves by means of experiments. It is not sufficient merely to talk of familiar instances observed outside the school, such as tramway metals, etc. Numerous examples may be found in the school-room or playground, the lines of the building, brickwork, floor, ceiling, etc. The children may be called upon in turn to draw the results of their observation on the blackboard.

The following facts should be elicited and may be illustrated best in a large hall.

(1) *Horizontal lines* lying in the same or independent planes which are *parallel to each other and recede* appear to converge in the same point—such as the parallel lines of the floor, ceiling, walls or furniture.

(2) The points of convergence lie in a common horizontal line—called the *Eye-level.*

(3) *The height of the eye-level varies with the height of the spectator.* This may be demonstrated by altering the height of the eye by changing from a sitting to a standing position or mounting on a stool.

(4) *Non-receding parallel lines* are represented as geometrically parallel. This fact should be elicited by placing the scholars in line so that the line of sight of each is at right angles to long parallel lines such as those of the floor, wall or ceiling.

(5) *The more remote an object the smaller it appears.* It follows that intervals between regularly placed objects also appear to diminish as they recede.

The following facts may be deduced at a later stage:—

(6) Parallel receding lines *inclined to the ground* appear to converge above or below the eye-level according as they *ascend* or *descend* from the spectator. Beginners often find this latter condition difficult to determine. It is referred to again (Art. 109).

(7) *All lines* (whatever their direction in relation to the ground) *which are parallel to the picture plane* are drawn in their *true* direction, hence if parallel to other lines they do not appear to converge. The fact that vertical lines are always represented as such, follows from this principle.

108. Drawing Exercises.—The following will be found a suitable course of exercises in drawing simple straight-lined objects.

The objects should be combined to form simple groups as proficiency is attained in drawing them individually. The position of the objects above the ground should be varied occasionally. They should be drawn in their normal position; thus, a bird-cage should be suspended *above* the eye-level.

Memory Drawing should be regularly practised in conjunction with these exercises.

Simple shading should be encouraged at an early stage. The few necessary lessons in shading will be well repaid by the increased interest in and accuracy of the drawings (see Chapter X.).

(1) A *cupboard or room-door* (Fig. 86) first represented closed, without foreshortening, and next open.   The panels and thickness of the wood may be drawn at a later stage.

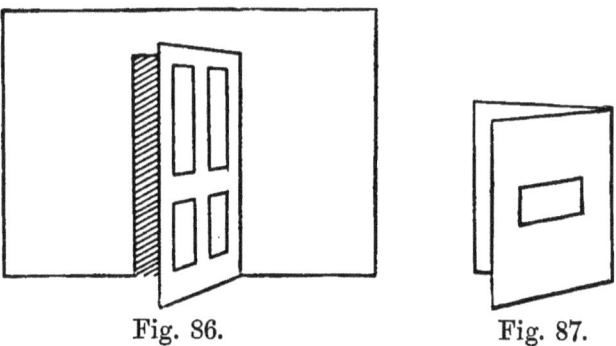

Fig. 86.   Fig. 87.

Suitable models in duplicate may be made of cardboard, so that each child may obtain the approximate view desired by the teacher.   See the book-cover or portfolio (Fig. 87).

(2) *The horizontal rectangular plane* may be taken next. (A large drawing-board, blackboard or card will serve.) The corners *b* and *c*, Fig. 88, should be placed first, and

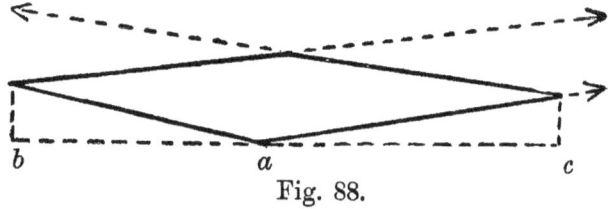

Fig. 88.

the proportionate distance between *ab* and *ac* marked previous to drawing the near adjacent edges to the right or left.   The angle of recedence of these lines may be gauged by means of a horizontal line and verified, after drawing, by means of "covering lines."

Parallel receding lines should always be drawn as long as the paper will admit to ensure their proper convergence. Strict attention must be paid to the *direction* of such lines rather than to their quality.

The apparatus described for circular planes (Art. 93) may be profitably employed for drawing square or rectangular planes.

(3) *Horizontal and vertical planes combined.*—Fig. 89 shows two useful models placed in various positions. They can easily be made of cardboard or wood, or parts of boxes will serve the purpose.

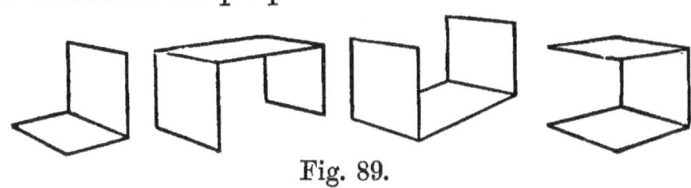

Fig. 89.

(4) *Rectangular solids* (in easy positions).—Cubes, square prisms, and objects based on them, such as bricks, boxes with lids closed or opened vertically or horizontally, or sliding lids partially drawn out; blocks of wood, " square-shaped " (tied with string or tape) lying horizontally or on end; simple articles of furniture such as a school form, child's stool. Simple architectural features (suitable for memory drawing), *e.g.* projecting doorstep, window-sill; roadway showing pavement and kerbs, railway platform. The following type models and objects based on them may be taken *after* those dealt with in the next chapter.

(5) *The square pyramid.*—When placed upright, it is necessary to represent the axis so that the apex may be obtained vertically over the centre of the base.

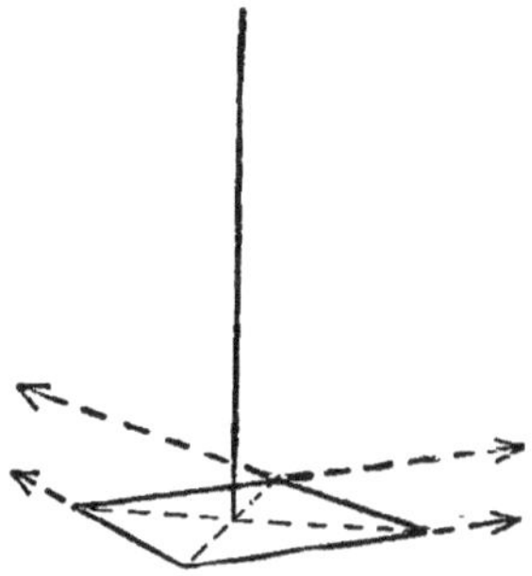

A simple model consisting of a square cardboard or wood plane, with a rod attached perpendicularly

Fig. 90.

at its centre, may be employed for first practice (Fig. 90).

(6) *The triangular prism.*—The rectangular base, 1, 2, 3, 4 (Fig. 91), should be drawn first in every case when this is horizontal (parallel to the ground). The near triangular end by means of its altitude (5–6), which is of course represented vertical. The nearer inclined edges,

1–6, 4–7, of the parallel ends must be made to converge upwards when they recede from the picture plane.

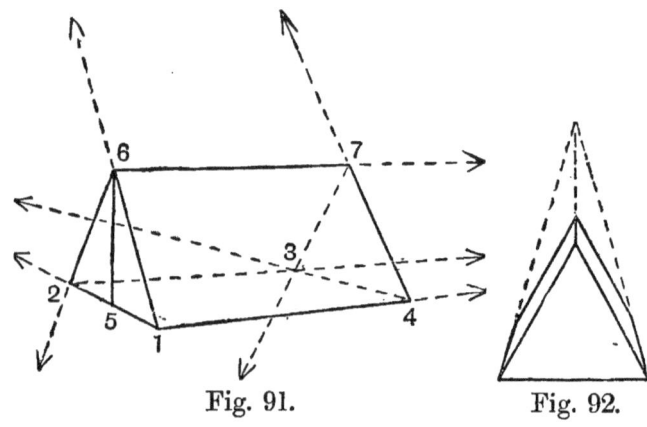

Fig. 91.   Fig. 92.

The ends of the triangular prism (Fig. 92) are parallel to the picture plane, and consequently retain their true form, and the corresponding edges of their ends are represented geometrically parallel to each other.

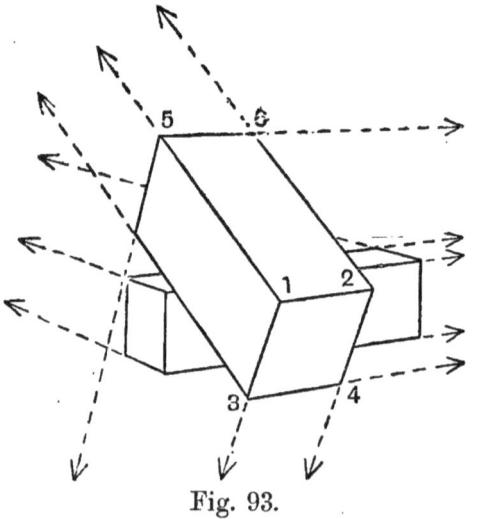

109. Ascending and Descending Lines.—Difficulty is experienced frequently in determining in which direction oblique parallel lines such as 1–6, 4–7, and 6–2, 7–3 (Fig. 91) converge. The direction is indicated by means of

Fig. 93.

arrows. The former are said to be *ascending* lines and converge *upwards*, and the latter descending lines and converge *downwards*.

A line is said to *ascend* when its nearer extremity is *lower* than the further one, and to *descend* when its near extremity is *higher*. Thus, in the view of the tilted square prism (Fig. 93), 1-5 and 2-6 are *Ascending* lines, and 1-3 and 2-4 are *Descending* lines. Lines 5-6, 1-2, and 3-4 are horizontal lines parallel to the long edges of the lower prism and converge with them.

Interesting objects based on the triangular prism and introducing oblique planes may easily be found, thus,

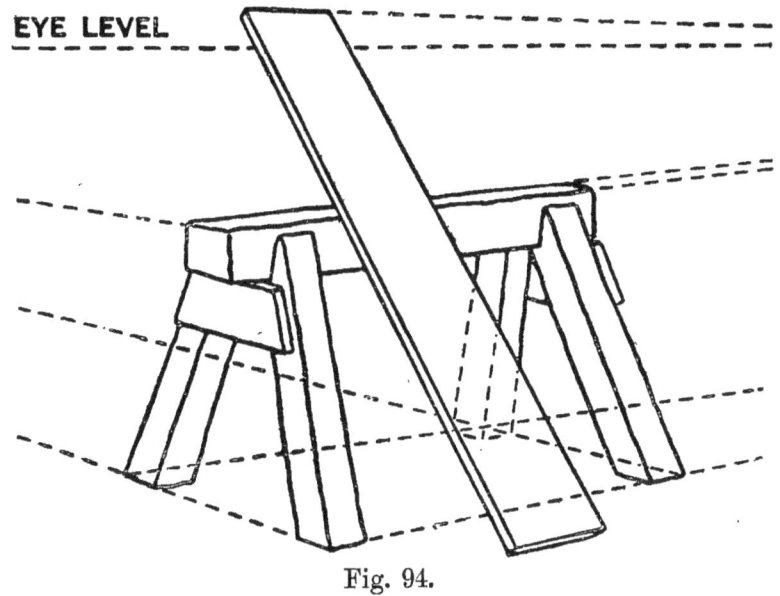

EYE LEVEL

Fig. 94.

large books, partly open, resting on their long edges or ends. Objects from the manual training shops form useful groups for advanced drawing, such as a sawing stool and plank (Fig. 94), smoothing plane and wooden mallet, etc., boxes with obliquely-open lids, a short ladder or pair of steps.

The *pyramid and triangular prism* are useful type models when dealing with architectural forms, such as roofs and steeples of buildings. The *hexagonal prism*, being a rare type form and therefore of little practical value, has been omitted.

CHAPTER IX.

PERSPECTIVE OF CIRCLES AND OTHER CURVES IN MORE DIFFICULT POSITIONS.

The search for form through true construction is the first basis of an artist's work.—G. CLAUSEN, R.A.

110. The Circle.—The representation of the foreshortened appearance of the circle when lying in a horizontal plane by a symmetrical curve, an ellipse, is applied to the drawing of the circle in *any* plane.

The cylinder as the type model and the numerous objects based thereon will afford ample practice.

111. Demonstration.—A pair of large wheels of equal size, with simple spokes and connected by a straight

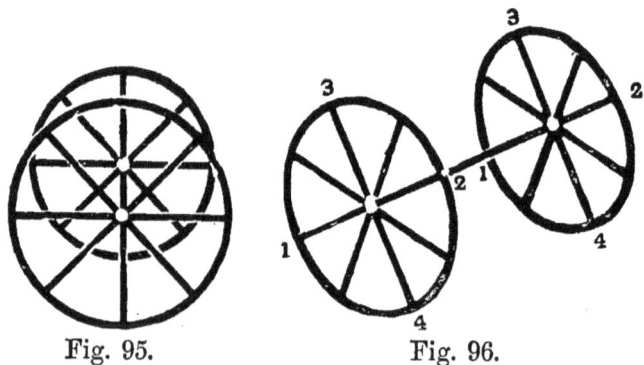

Fig. 95.   Fig. 96.

axle may be placed below the eye-level of the children, so that the wheels are perpendicular and the rod parallel to the ground. The class may be ranged round the object. Two cardboard discs connected by a rod may be used if the wheels are not available.

The following facts should be elicited : (1) The diameters of the respective circles (each made up by a pair of spokes) appear to be equal when the plane of the circle is at right angles to the line of sight (Fig. 95). Otherwise, (2) They vary in length as the planes of the circles recede. The shortest diameter, *e.g.* 1–2, Fig. 96 and Fig. 97, is that which is in the line of the axis connecting the circles, while the longest, 3–4, always appears geometrically at right angles to it. Each of these, major and minor diameters, divides the circle into two symmetrical parts. This holds good, no matter in what position the model lies, whether vertical, horizontal or oblique.

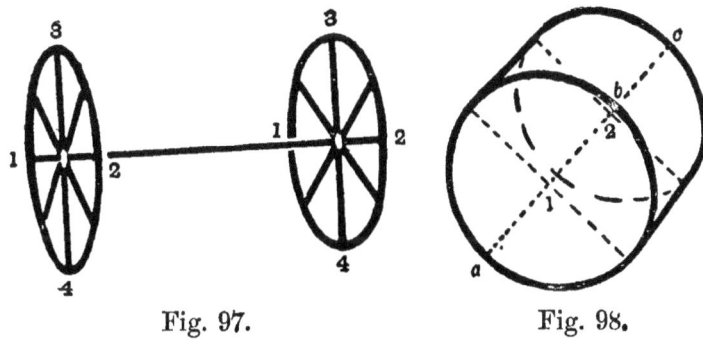

Fig. 97.   Fig. 98.

The Cylinder (lying horizontally) is drawn on the same principle as the above model.

The axis, 1–2 (Fig. 98), may be drawn first. This being an imaginary line, however, it will be found easier to begin by drawing the straight lines representing the sides of the cylinder and which converge when either end is in view. Care must be taken that these straight lines are drawn tangentially to the curves of the ends.

The pencil may be employed occasionally in order to *test the judgment* as to the apparent degree of curvature of the ends or their direction or proportions, as when dealing with purely straight-lined forms. Thus, the proportion between the minor diameter *a-b* of the near end of the cylinder (Fig. 98) and the extreme length *a-c* should be carefully noted. The pencil in this case must be held *inclined* to the ground, so as to *cover* the line of the axis, but not to recede with it.

The numerous common objects of cylindrical form, such as jars, pans, etc., already mentioned (Chaps. VI. and VII.), may now be drawn in positions other than upright.

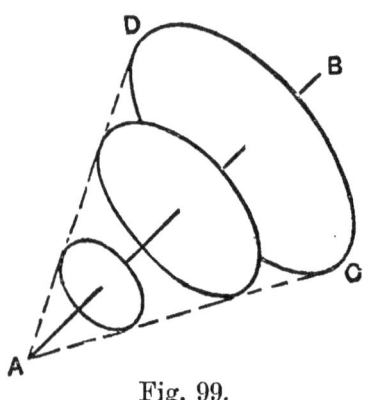

Fig. 99.

112. The Cone, Truncated Cone, and Objects Based thereon.—(More difficult positions.)

The disc and rod apparatus (see Art. 96) may be employed when introducing new and more difficult positions, such as the cone or truncated cone lying on its side.

The axis (AB, Fig. 99) of these solids is drawn geometrically bisecting the angle, DAC, made by the lines representing the "sides." Otherwise the method of procedure is the same as in the case of the cylinder.

113. Objects with Handles, Spouts, or other Attachments.—These forms, being common and affording good practice in drawing, may be studied as a group. The drawing must always be planned carefully, the children being encouraged to discover the best method of procedure for themselves by handling the object and noting peculiarities of its construction. The type models should be reverted to wherever possible.

Especial care is necessary when dealing with details when these are comparatively small, such as the hook and eye attachment of a pail-handle. Owing to faulty observation there is usually a tendency to slur over such parts or omit them altogether. Large analogous forms can be employed, or models of small parts made on a larger scale of cardboard, wire, tin, etc., and drawn. Thus a suspended meat-hook or large, bent piece of stout wire (Fig. 100) might be drawn before dealing with the pail-handle. A small hoop or cardboard disc with three or four pairs of cardboard or paper " eyes " attached will represent the mouth of the pail (Fig. 101).

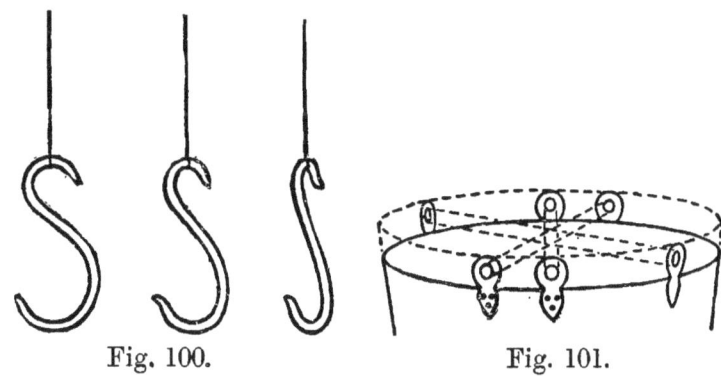

Fig. 100.   Fig. 101.

A beginning may be made with a simple wire handle such as that of a beer-can (Fig. 102). The relative position of the pair of fastenings obviously depends in

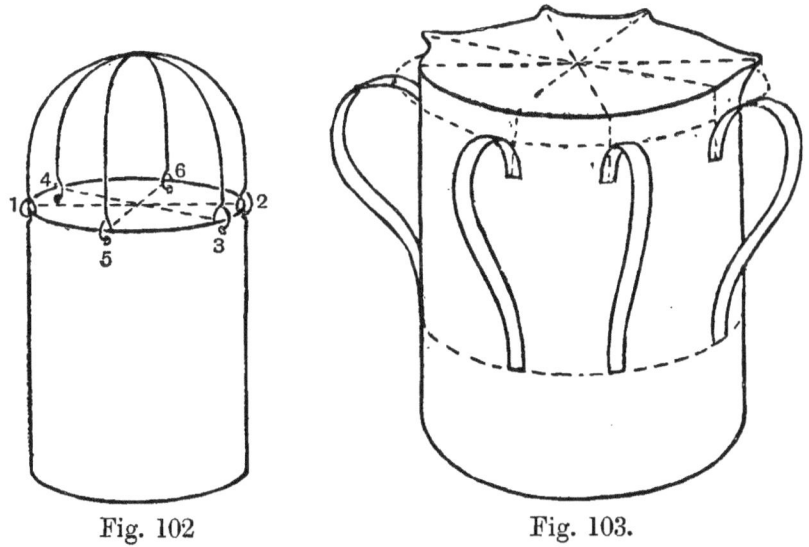

Fig. 102   Fig. 103.

every case on a diameter of the circular opening of the can (whether the handle is vertical or inclined), as 1-2, 3–4, 5–6. The same principle applies to the "placing" of

the handle and spout of the can (Fig. 103), and a more
extended application is shown in the alignment of the
lower handle and the spout of the watering can (Fig. 104).

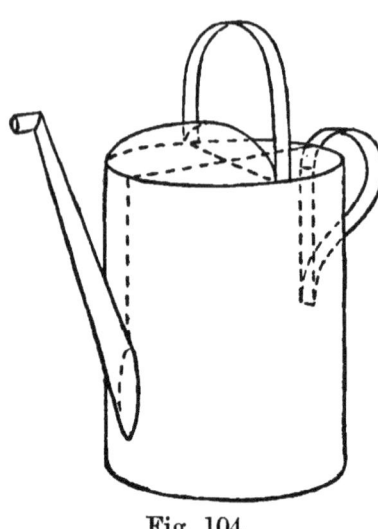

The horizontal portion of the
spout is parallel to the diameter marking the position of
the spout and handle at-
tached to the body of the
can, and this diameter is per-
spectively at right angles to
that of the vertical handle.

Separate studies of tin
handles may also be made
from large models, as in the
case of the wire handle.

**114. Advanced Object
Drawing.**—In concluding
this section a few words

Fig. 104.

must be added concerning
the large number of objects
that do not conform entirely to any particular type. Such
objects, especially natural ones, with their more subtle
effects of perspective, though often extremely difficult, are
most interesting. They should be studied concurrently
with the more formal objects described. The principles
and methods evolved from the study of the latter may be
applied continually.

General Hints.—View the object with half-closed eye,
until the sense of looking at a *picture* rather than a concrete form is produced. Try to forget, at this stage, the
existence of details. Imagine the form "flattened out"
or projected in silhouette.

Set out the proportions and pose of the object by means
of a few light strokes.

Do not let the *known* proportions or shape of an object
influence the judgment as to its particular appearance.
Thus, observe the varied appearance of the pipe (Fig. 105)
as turned about in the writer's hand. Position 1 shows
the object in elevation and in its true proportions, the

length being much greater than its height; in Position 2, however, it appears to be less.   Again, in Position 3 the

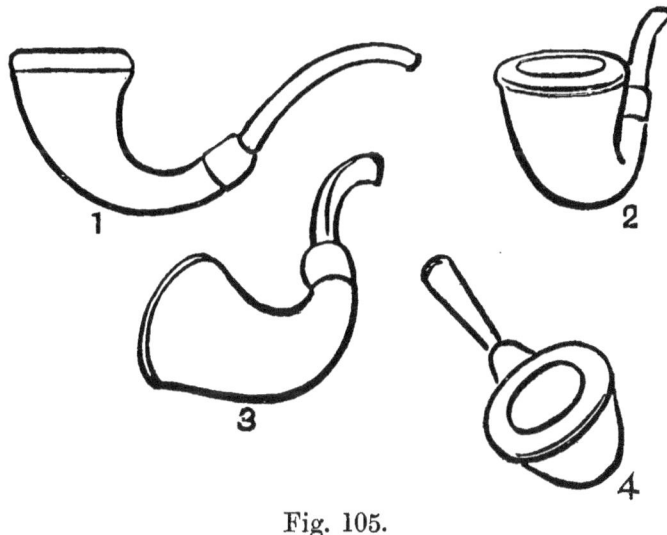

Fig. 105.

stem and mouthpiece show decided and characteristic curves which are entirely lost in Position 4.

CHAPTER X.

LIGHT AND SHADE.

*All drawing depends primarily on your power of representing Roundness. . . . For Nature is made up of roundnesses; not the roundnesses of perfect globes, but of variously curved surfaces. Boughs are rounded, leaves are rounded, stones are rounded, cheeks are rounded, and curls are rounded: there is no more flatness in the natural world than there is vacancy.—*RUSKIN.

115. Reasons for Teaching.—The study of light and shade is too often neglected in elementary art teaching. The chief cause, probably, is the unsuitable lighting of the classroom, while the difficulty of finding a simple technique often prevents teachers from introducing the subject at an early stage.

It is important, however, that these difficulties should be surmounted, for light and shade is an essential truth in the representation of objects, which we cannot afford to ignore, and which adds threefold to the interest of drawing. The beauty of objects often depends more on the play of light and shade than on form, and a skilful arrangement in lighting will change quite commonplace objects into beautiful artistic studies. We know how patiently photographers will wait for hours or even days to see certain light and shade effects.

As soon as a pupil is able to represent the form of a simple object he should be shown a method of indicating its solidity; it is inadvisable to wait until the form is perfect before light and shade is attempted, for it is the light and shade which indicates the form. A light and shade drawing teaches the pupil to appreciate mass as well as contour.

116. The Difficulty of Lighting.—For elementary studies in light and shade the object should be lighted in one direction only and this from the side. In classrooms where the lighting is unsuitable, apparatus must be devised. A large wooden box from which two sides have been

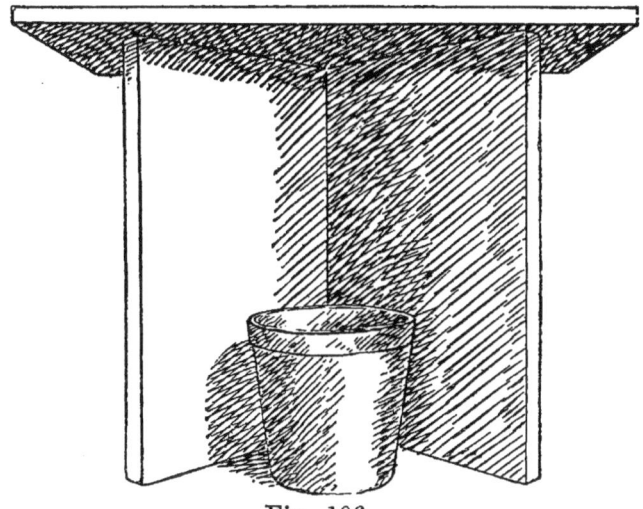

Fig. 106.

removed, or an arrangement of three drawing boards will be found effective (see Fig. 106). The upper board may be arranged to stop the light from above, while the side boards may be so placed that the object is lighted mainly from one side. Artificial light gives greater definition to the shadows, for daylight is more diffused and weakens the darker portions. A suitable background to which the various tones can be related should usually be provided. This will materially assist in defining the contour of the objects. A drawing board or sheet of paper (white or tinted) placed in a vertical position behind the objects can be easily arranged.

117. Steps in Teaching.—The pupil must be taught to see. This is especially necessary in light and shade drawing. There is a danger of indicating shade in a mechanical way according to the teacher's directions, but every copy should be the result of real observation by individual pupils. Here lies the teacher's chief difficulty. He must be extremely careful that his own illustrations are not copied. It will be necessary in the early stages to spend a considerable part of the time devoted to light and shade in leading the scholars to realise the full meaning of their visual impressions.

The forms of objects are seen not by outline but by contrast of light and shade, and these terms are only relative, for a dark object may be light when placed against a darker one, and a light object dark when compared with a lighter one. The pupils must decide which part of the object appears lightest and which darkest before they begin to shade. *If the eyes are nearly closed* the shade on objects becomes more apparent, and by looking through a small hole in brown or black paper the various tones may be more easily compared. The shape of the cast shadow must be carefully studied, as this helps to decide the shape of the object casting the shadow, as well as the shape and nature of the surface receiving the same.

118. Exercises in Technique.—It is well to begin with line shading in pencil. Exercises in drawing parallel lines in various directions to fill certain spaces will give

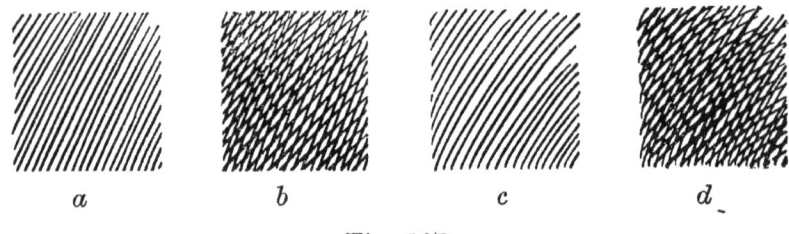

a   b   c   d

Fig. 107.

facility. The lines should be drawn quickly and freely, care being taken that they do not run beyond the set space. Similar exercises with the pen will help to secure careful and exact work. In "cross-hatching" the lines should not cross at right angles, but should form little spaces of the diamond pattern. The lines may be straight or curved to suit the contour of the object (Fig. 107).

Crayon or charcoal may be used in a similar way.

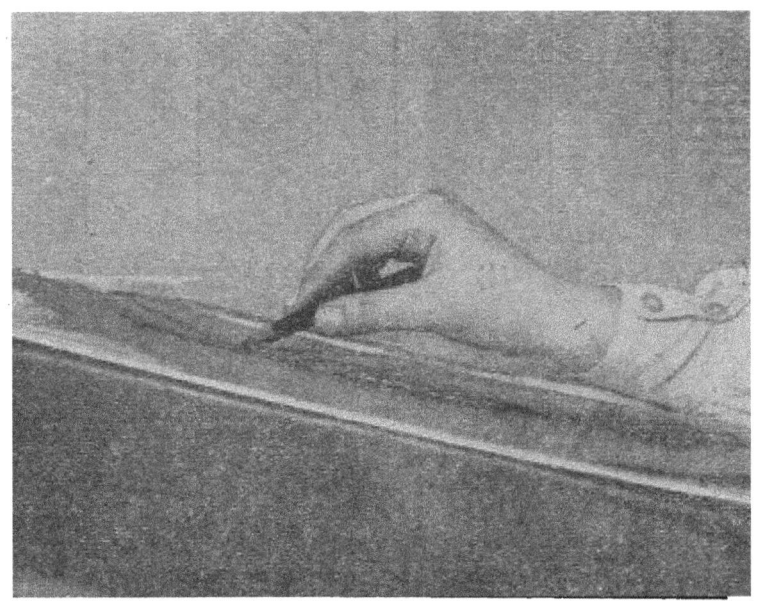

Fig. 108.
Method of holding crayon and charcoal.

The following diagrams illustrate various methods of indicating gradation of tone in line shading (Fig. 109).

(*a*) Lines of shade are placed closer together to indicate the darker shade; the lines may be made thicker in the darkest part.

(*b*) Parallel lines with spaces of equal width are used; but each line is made to diminish in thickness by removing the pressure. In this method the pencil or crayon is held under the hand and the side of the point is used (see Fig. 108).

(*c*) The same method is adopted as in (*a*), but here two series of straight lines cross at an acute angle.

(*d*) As in (*c*), but lines are curved to indicate gradation on curved surfaces.

The method of shading by means of powdered chalk and paper stumps is not suitable for the elementary stages;

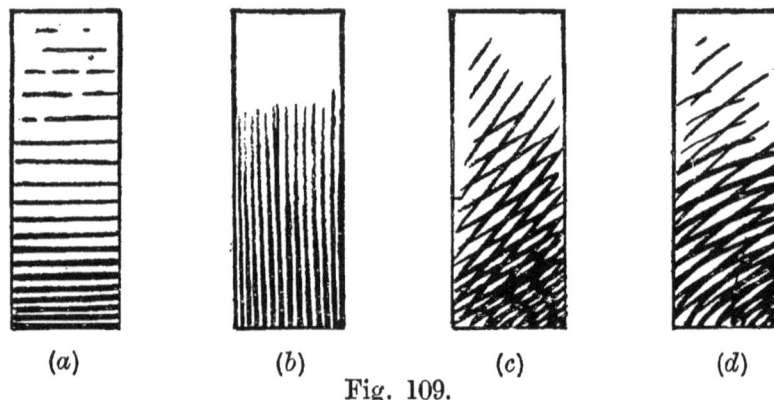

(a)   (b)   (c)   (d)

Fig. 109.

the technique is not easy and can only be used satisfactorily by advanced pupils.

119. First Exercises in Shading from Objects.—

It is a good plan to begin the study of light and shade by a few lessons on rectangular objects. It is true there is a difficulty in drawing the outline correctly, but the planes of shade are well marked and easily distinguished by

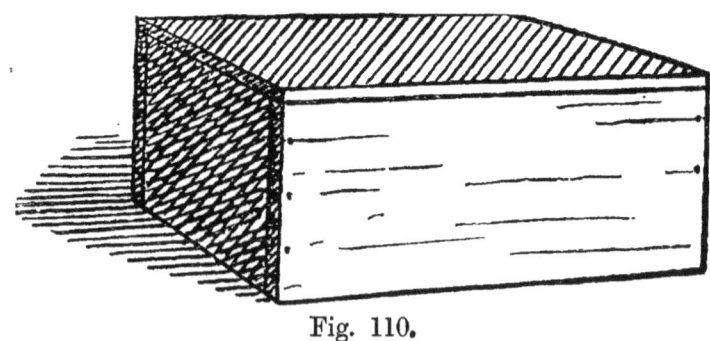

Fig. 110.

beginners. Gradation in tone may be omitted in the early exercises, and attention given mainly to the three or four distinct planes of shade.

When the pupils understand what to look for and how
to represent what they see, the ordinary course of object
drawing may be fol-
lowed. Such an exercise
as the shading of a box
may be carried out by
pencil or crayon lines
and is suitable for
brushwork. The planes
of shade can be shown
by using várying shades
of the same colour (see Arts. 51 and 54).

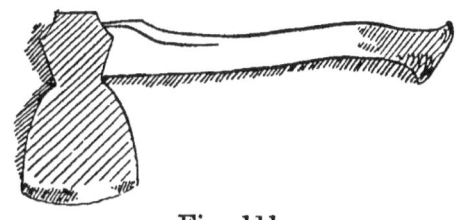

Fig. 111.

As soon as the pupil can draw a simple object he should
be allowed to indicate the darker parts by using parallel
lines. He should be encouraged to draw the cast shadow
whenever one is visible (see Fig. 111).

Shading of Cylindrical Objects, *e.g.* a gingerbeer
bottle.

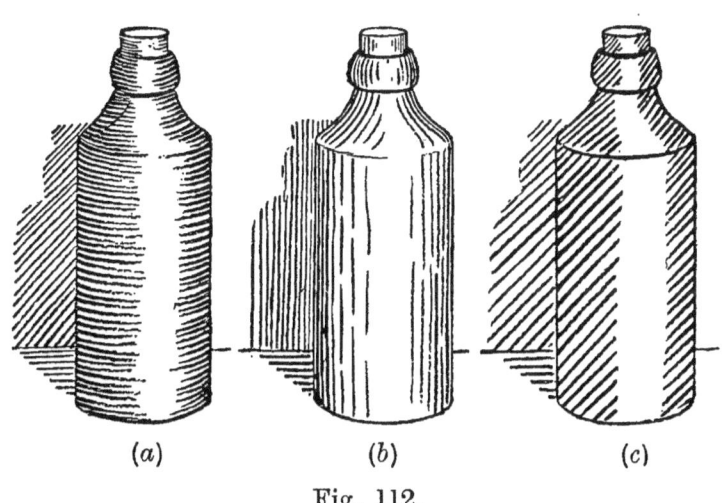

(a)   (b)   (c)

Fig. 112.

The object must be drawn carefully in outline, together
with the shadow. The darker portions may be boldly
shaded by parallel lines—

(a) *Curved,* to follow the horizontal curvature, the lines

made thicker at darkest portion—the pencil may be held under the hand (see Fig. 108).

(*b*) *Upright and curved*, to follow the vertical contour —the lines closer together at the darkest portion.

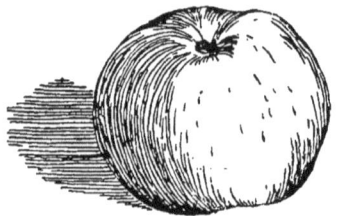

(*c*) *Straight lines at an angle of about* 45°. These lines may be thicker in the darkest portions.

The lines indicating the cast shadow should also show the direction of the surface on which the shadow falls, thus in the

Fig. 113.

illustration the horizontal surface is best shown by horizontal lines (see Fig. 112).

120. Shading from Natural Objects such as fruits, shells, leaves, etc., may be introduced as soon as pupils can draw them fairly well. In such objects the lines of shade should follow the contour, and thus assist in showing solidity as well as curvature (Fig. 113).

A flower study in pencil may be improved by shading the background (Fig. 114). If pen and ink is used, the pencil outline may be dispensed with and a more truthful result secured. The method is very effective in the case of white flowers, such as snowdrop, lily, narcissus, daisy, clematis, camellia, etc.

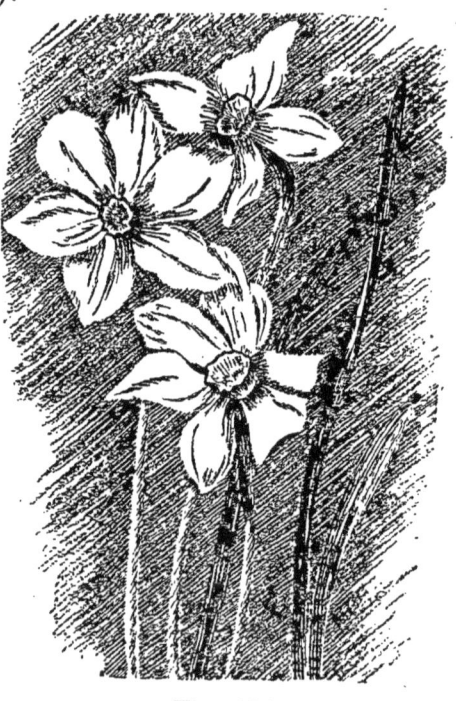

Fig. 114.

121. Exercises on Brown or Tinted Paper.— Children take much delight is using crayons to represent objects. They are able to show approximate colour as well as light and shade. The crayons should be held under the hand (see Fig. 108) and used lightly; the various tones may be produced by cross-hatching (see Fig. 107) and the colours may be blended as explained in Art. 24.

Black and white crayons are most effective in representing bright reflecting surfaces such as glass, metal or earthenware. The object is sketched in outline with either crayon and the darkest portions are shaded first. The rubber should not be used, as it smudges the crayon and spoils the effect. The bright spots or streaks are reserved for the final touches with the white crayons.

The following exercises are especially suitable for homework :—

> *Glass objects:*—jug, tumbler, bottle, dish, vase.
> *Metal objects:*—teapot, canister, biscuit-barrel, lamp.
> *Earthenware:*—cup, saucer, jug, basin, vase.
> *Drapery:*—handkerchief, duster (suspended).

Coloured crayons may be used for such objects as fruits, crockery, books, matchboxes, vases, etc. In all these exercises attention should be given to artistic grouping and arrangement. The background and cast shadow should always be considered and general effects preferred to details.

122. Drawing in Light and Shade from Casts can only be introduced where arrangements are made so that not more than two pupils study from the same cast. Unless the desks are properly set out and the room correctly lighted the exercises become too complicated and quite beyond the powers of elementary scholars.

CHAPTER XI.

THE DRAWING OF ORNAMENT, INCLUDING DESIGN.

Invention is one of the great marks of genius; but if we consult experience, we shall find that it is by being conversant with the inventions of others that we learn to invent, as by reading the thoughts of others we learn to think.

Sir Joshua Reynolds.

123. Special Advantages.—These exercises give training in drawing large regular curves, such as circles and spirals, which involve the use of muscles of the wrist and forearm. This advantage will be entirely lost if pupils are allowed to make small drawings. Large sheets of drawing paper pinned to boards should be used.

Training in the judgment of proportion is more definite than in nature drawing; mistakes are more easily detected both by teacher and pupil.

The Principles of Beauty explained in Chapter V. will be found to agree with the Principles of Ornament. The practical value of this knowledge will be apparent in the design exercises.

The study of good ornament is a necessary preparation for lessons in design. Exercises on adaptation of form and planning of designs will give scope for invention and originality, but the teacher must not expect pupils to contrive valuable designs until their minds are well stored with natural forms. It is well, therefore, to leave design until a later stage, although in this course suggestions are given for combining design with the study of ornament at each stage.

Lessons showing how conventional forms are derived from nature will lead to interest in ornament and consequently an appreciation of fitting decoration. If pupils are permitted to paint their drawings the importance of well-balanced spaces of colour will be apparent and a study of colour harmony will follow.

124. The Use of Copies in the Study of Ornament.
—As a rule drawings from diagrams or pictures should not be made until sufficient knowledge has been obtained to appreciate the inner meaning of the lines used; hence the inadvisability of using them for the youngest pupils. We should not attempt to prejudice the child's mind in favour of certain generally accepted renderings of form; we blunt his powers of observation thereby.

125. Specimens of Applied Ornament.—As far as possible actual specimens of ornament should be available in order to show pupils the practical use of the work they are doing. In some cases these specimens can be copied directly by the scholars. Ornamental objects of earthenware, such as jugs, cups, vases, etc.; of wood, such as panels, furniture, boxes; of iron, and of plaster can be obtained. Specimens of wallpaper, bookcovers, tapestry, and lace would be useful.

Pupils should be instructed to notice various kinds of ornament in their homes and in the street, and occasionally asked to prepare a specimen to be drawn from memory.

126. Classification of Copies.—Copies of some kind will be necessary for a systematic study of the subject, and the teacher should see that the ornament is selected either for its beauty or its historical value.

Large copy by teacher on blackboard.—The copy is built up step by step, and enables the child to follow an orderly and detailed plan of construction.

Large printed diagram placed on easel before class.—In this case the pupils should be questioned with regard to proportion, method of procedure, etc., before they begin to draw. Such questions as :—

Which way will you place your paper? Why?
Which is the widest part of the copy?
Which line will you draw first? Which next? Etc.

Note.—Care must be taken to ensure that each pupil gets a full view of the diagram. If necessary, the copy should be duplicated.

A smaller copy for each pupil.—This is the most convenient method; the pupil can study his example more closely. If all the pupils are provided with the same copy, general mistakes can be more easily pointed out and illustrated on the blackboard. Copies can be traced and reproduced on the hectograph or cyclostyle; such copies have been found to answer admirably.

Photographs of ornament may be used in advanced stages, but here again it is an advantage for each scholar to have the same copy.

SCHEME OF LESSONS.

127. Stage I.—Easy Ornamental Forms consisting of straight lines and easy curves.
Simple Leaf Forms. Shield Shapes (see Art. 39).

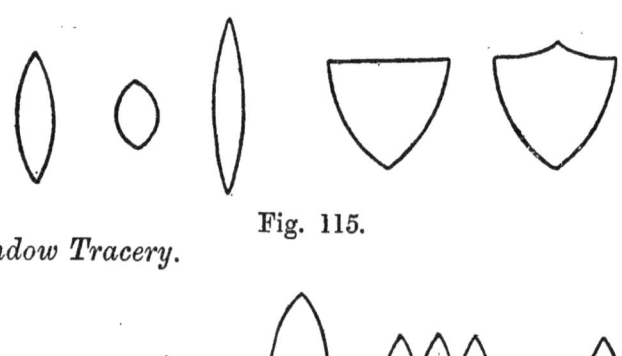

Window Tracery.

Fig. 115.

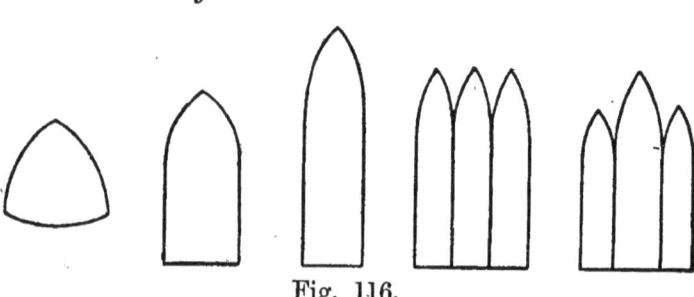

Fig. 116.

Plain Lettering—large and small.

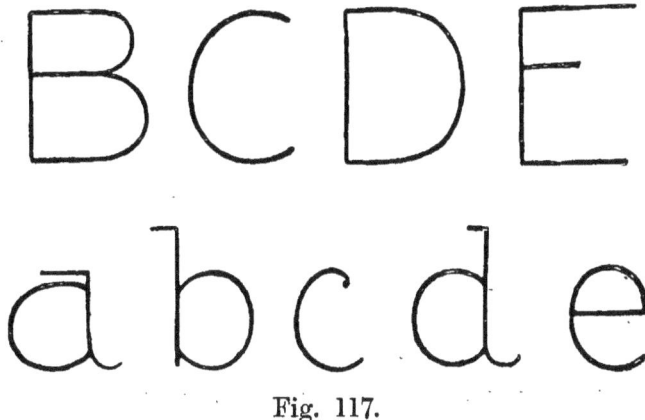

Fig. 117.

NOTES.

It is a good plan to allow a pupil to draw on blackboard while the class watches. The teacher may stand by, sometimes to suggest, sometimes to criticise, but more often to question the class on method of procedure.

Use very few construction lines in these copies. In order that corresponding points may be exactly opposite, the pencil should be moved across the paper, but no line need be drawn: pupils must be trained to depend upon the eye alone for measuring.

Exercises in Design.—(Compass, ruler, and set square will be necessary.)

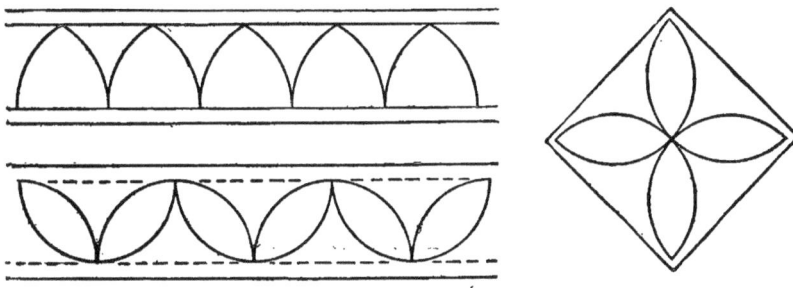

Fig. 118.

1. The construction and harmonious division into spaces of the following geometrical figures :—triangle, square, rectangle, rhombus, circle, semicircle, etc.

2. Repetition of straight-lined forms, construction of borders and frames. These may be used in decorating homework books, etc.

3. Repetition of simple curves and leaf forms to fill borders and given spaces (see Fig. 118).

128. Stage II.—Ornament derived from Leaf and Petal Forms, including compound curves and simple spirals.

Leaf and petal forms.
Bent-iron work patterns of similar form.

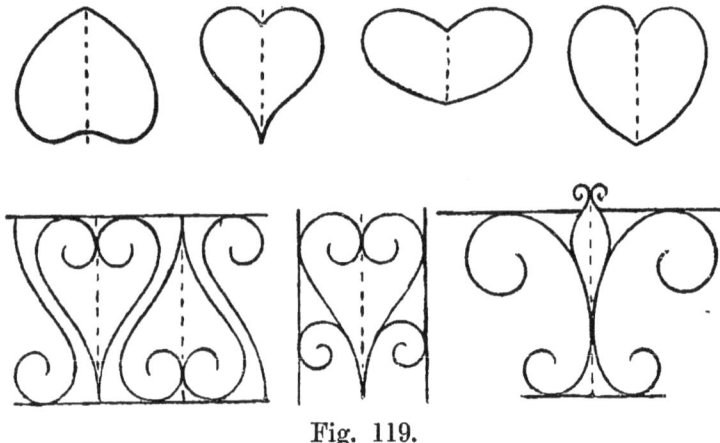

Fig. 119.

Ornamental lettering, introducing spiral.

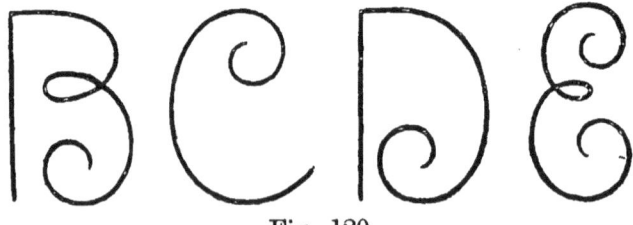

Fig. 120.

Ornamental rosettes ; how derived from wild rose (see Model Lesson, Art. 129). The pupils may now be set to design rosettes, etc., to fill various shapes, based on this and other natural forms (Fig. 121).

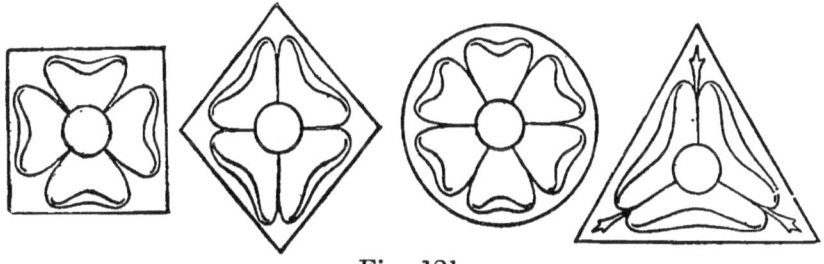

Fig. 121.

Scrolls are useful for ornamentation.

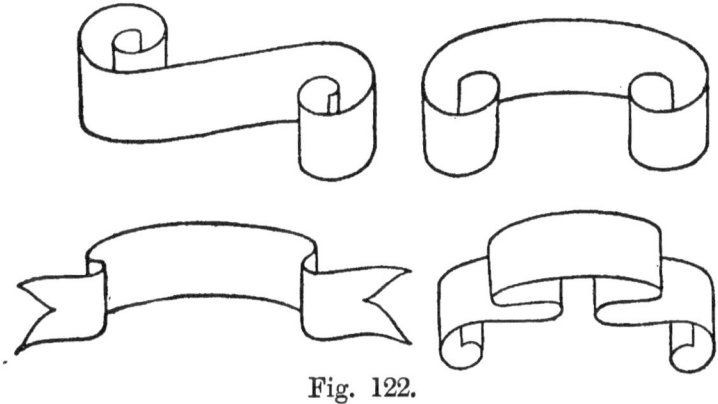

Fig. 122.

129. Model Lesson. "The Construction of a Rosette."—The wild rose has been studied from Nature. The circular form in the full view of the flower, the heart-shaped petals and the general balance have been specially pointed out. The teacher explains that he wishes to convert the form of a natural rose into ornament, and in order to do this he must make the petals regular in curvature, equal in size, and fit them into a perfect circle. Selected pupils are allowed to construct the circle on the blackboard (see Art. 42). The teacher then shows the class how this circle may be divided into five equal parts by judgment. The pupils now copy the circle with the five divisions. One petal should be sketched on the board; the necessity for balancing the same on one of the radiating lines must be pointed out. The remaining petals are drawn on the board by selected pupils, who are warned to see that the petals exactly touch and do not overlap as

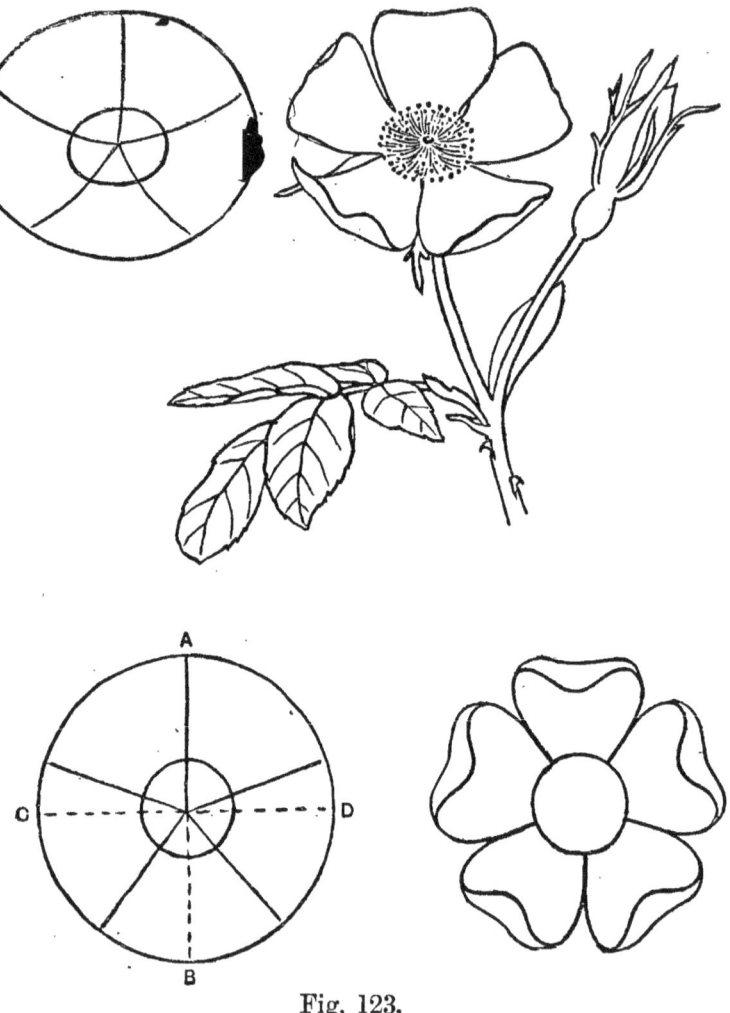

Fig. 123.

they sometimes do in the natural flower. The lines showing the curling of the petals may be omitted, but if inserted the teacher will take care that the junction with the edges of the petal are tangential. The beauty of this design depends upon Radiation and Repetition.

130. Stage III.—More Difficult Ornament, derived from leaf and flower forms.

Simple Ornamental Objects, such as vases, jugs, basins, etc., involving a study of compound curves found in such natural objects as bell-shaped flowers (Fig. 124). Lessons may be made interesting by comparing flowers of similar shape. The difficulty of balancing curves on an inclined line is introduced.

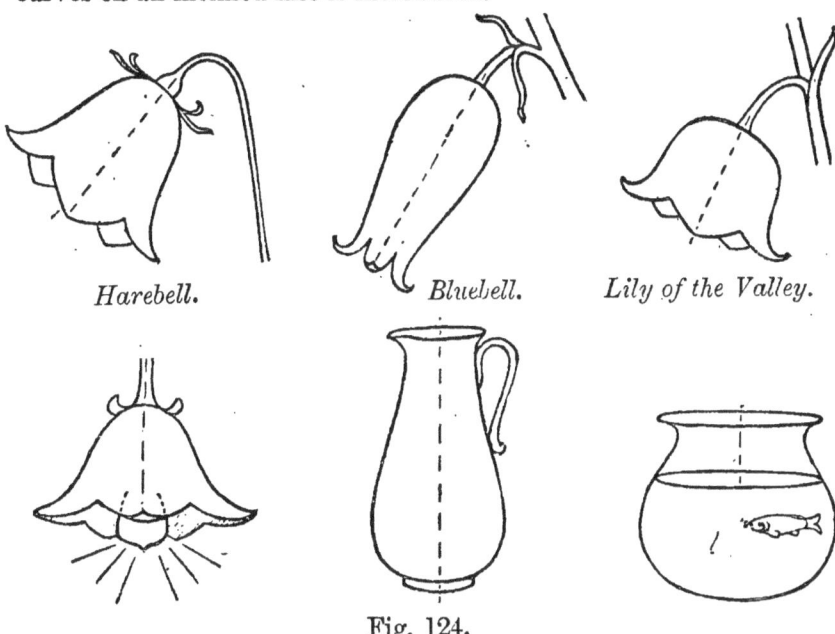

Harebell.　　　　Bluebell.　　　Lily of the Valley.

Fig. 124.

Exercises in Design, based on flower and leaf forms. These exercises (see Fig. 125) are specially suitable for colour work. The teacher may give the leading lines of a design to which the pupils are required to apply a given form, *e.g.* the harebell may be utilised to fill the spaces in Fig. 125*a.*

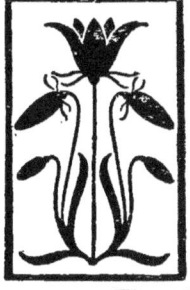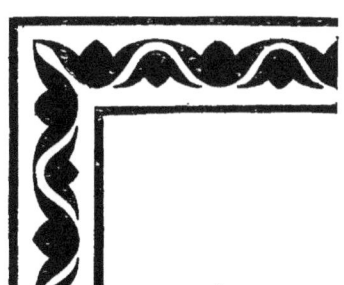

Fig. 125.

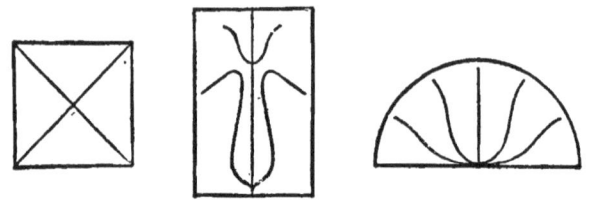

Fig. 125a.

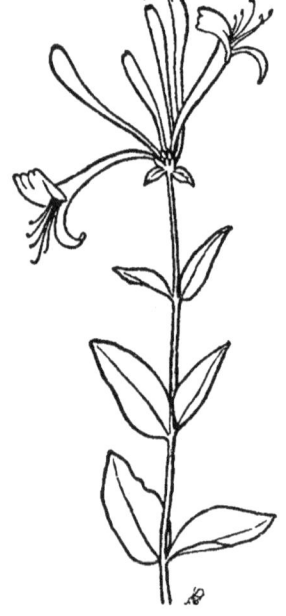

The Anthemion.—The anthemion (Fig. 126, *b*) is said to be derived from the honeysuckle. The Principles of Balance, Radiation, Repetition, Curvature, and Contrast are all illustrated. There are many forms of the ornament ; new forms may be designed by varying the shape and number of the petals.

(*a*)   (*b*)

Fig. 126.

Old English Lettering, drawn to large scale at first.

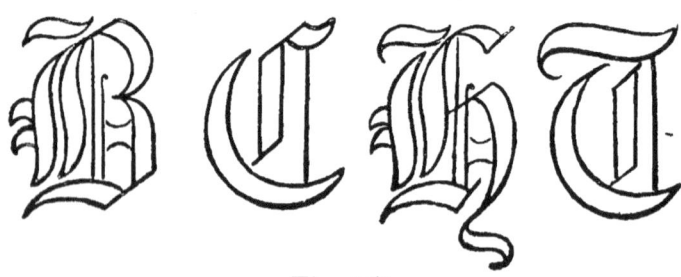

Fig. 127.

Miscellaneous Ornament, to be copied from actual material, such as :—

Patterns in iron work.　　Brackets of various material.
Designs on wallpaper.　　Patterns on textiles.
Ornamental frames.　　Ornament on household utensils.

Notes.—These exercises will be found especially suitable for homework. The selection of the design must necessarily be left to the pupil, and this will give an opportunity for his discrimination and taste. The teacher's criticism of the ornament chosen should be a valuable aid and serve to guide the pupil in a future choice.

The geometrical basis of some of these forms of ornament must be set out with instruments.

131. Stage IV.—Simple Classical Ornament, involving a further study of the spiral and acanthus leaf.

The Spiral in Nature and in Art.—This most beautiful curve is rarely found perfect in natural forms, but good specimens may be observed in shells, and in the tendrils of climbing plants (Fig. 128).

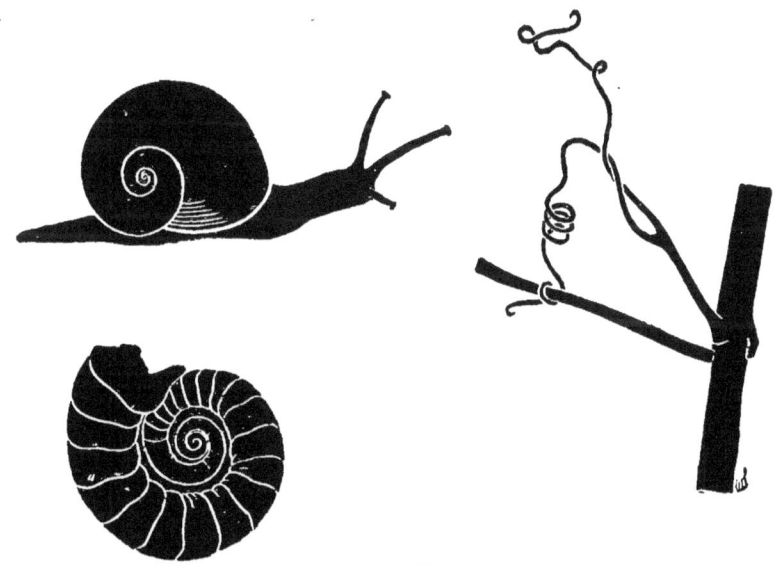

Fig. 128.

The dotted construction lines shown in Fig. 129, *a* may be used in the first exercises to show the position of the greatest width of each section of the curve. In later exercises the curve should be sketched without construction lines. The gradual diminution of the space between the lines as the centre is approached must be pointed out.

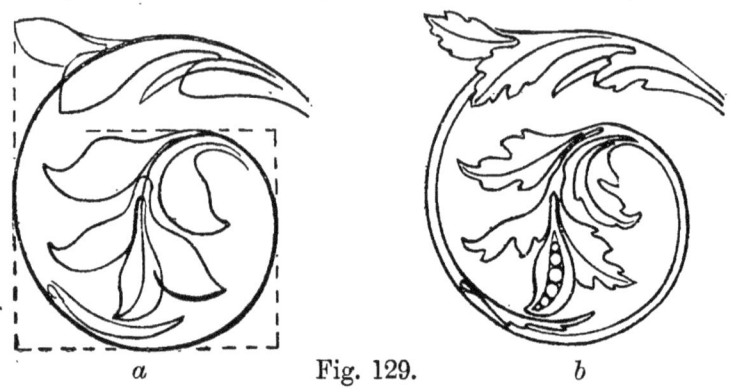

a   Fig. 129.   b

The decorative spirals of the Ionic column may be referred to and illustrated in this lesson.

The Acanthus Leaf.—No leaf has been used for ornamental purposes to a greater extent than the acanthus

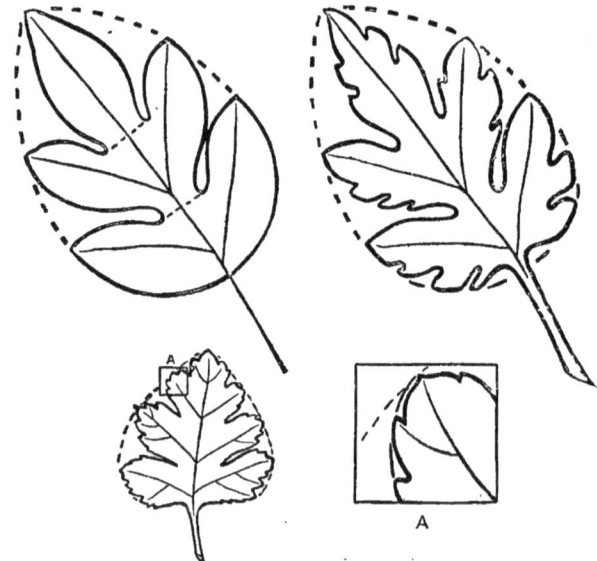

Fig. 130.

leaf (see Fig. 131). Its beauty depends chiefly on Curvature and Radiation. As we cannot easily obtain the natural leaf, it is suggested that leaves of the chrysanthemum and hawthorn should first be studied (see Fig. 130). Draw the acanthus leaf in the following order:—

1. Chief vein and general shape of whole leaf (see that this is correctly balanced).
2. Secondary veins and lobes which are similar in shape and construction to the leaf as a whole.
3. Serrations. These again are repetitions of the lobes and follow a definite form (cf. Fig. 130, A).

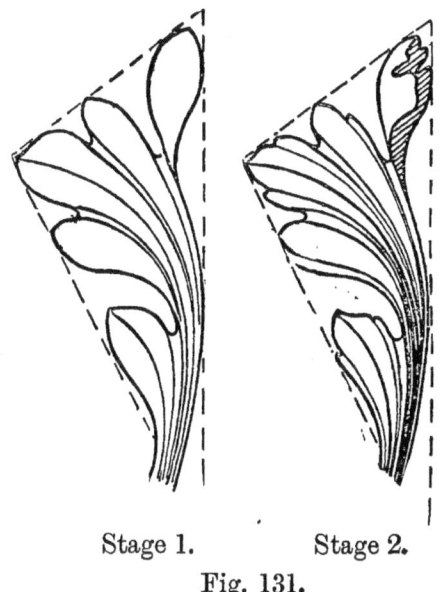

Stage 1.   Stage 2.

Fig. 131.

A picture or sketch of a Corinthian column showing the application of the ornament will be interesting in these lessons.

Miscellaneous Ornament, from the actual material (see Stage III., page 111).

Exercises in Design. — Geometrical designs based on flower forms. A flower should be studied from nature, simplified and adapted to fill various geometrical figures, such as circles, squares, triangles, etc. See Plate IV. This design has been executed in pencil and monochrome.

This design, the work of a pupil, might have been carried further by applying the natural colour of leaves and flowers and filling the centre panel with the flower in plan, etc.

Grotesque Ornament.—This may be made extremely interesting (see Ruskin's *Modern Painters,* Vol. III., Chap. 8).

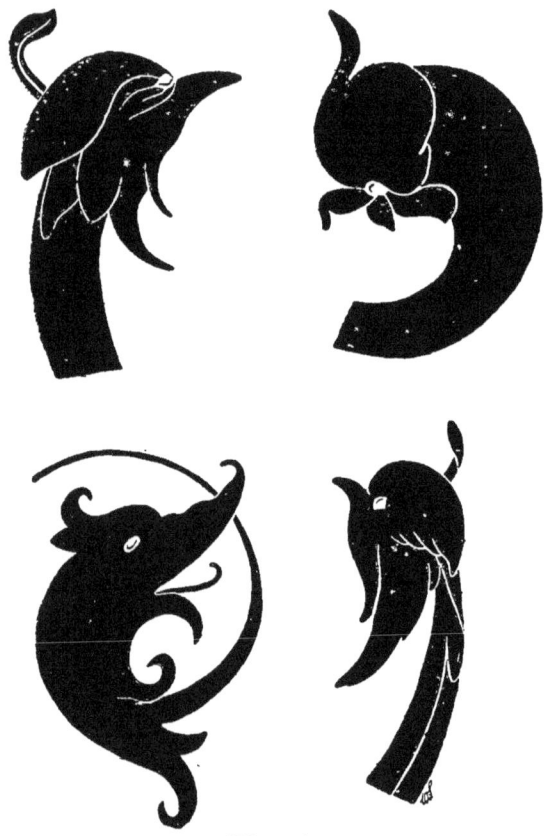

Fig. 132.

132. Stage IV.—Drawing from Photograph of Ornament, including Architecture, and from Specimens of Woodcarving, Textiles, Pottery, etc.

General Method :—1. Draw boundaries of ornament or of part to be studied in correct proportion.

2. Find out plan of leading lines and insert chief masses of the design; carefully study shapes and proportions of spaces.

Note.—Pupil should often hold his drawing in a vertical position at this stage to test balance, etc.

3. Insert detail of characteristic portions.

4. Finish with soft line in pencil, pen, or brush, taking care to preserve the fluency of curves and character of ornamental forms. By varying the thickness of line an expression of relief can be made—the nearer edges should be the thicker.

Note.—After the previous lessons pupils will be keen to discover examples of Radiation, Repetition, etc., and mistakes in these principles can easily be brought home to them.

Design Exercises as in Stage IV., with special reference to actual object decoration, *e.g.* greeting cards, programmes; design for door-knocker, book-cover, plate, linoleum, wallpaper; suitable decoration for a given vase, jug, iron stove, etc.

Architecture.—A study of the distinguishing features of the various orders of architecture will arouse interest in the construction and decoration of local buildings. Such lessons should be illustrated by photographs, pictures, and sketches, and may be made the basis of useful drawing lessons.

CHAPTER XII.

DRAWING FROM MEMORY AND IMAGINATION.

Invention, strictly speaking, is little more than a new combination of those images which have been previously gathered and deposited in the memory: nothing can come of nothing: he who has laid up no materials can produce no combinations.—SIR JOSHUA REYNOLDS.

133. Memory and Drawing.—Memory of form and the process of drawing are intimately connected. The mere act of copying a form which is actually present entails an effort of memory, since the form must be visualised and remembered while recording it. Faulty representation is often due to weakness in the latter respect as much as to weakness of execution.

Children sometimes even evade the process of memorising altogether. In map-drawing, for example, the coast-line is sometimes drawn on the paper while the eye follows the indentations marked in the copy. Unless checked, young children frequently trace the contours of objects in the same way. This method has as little value as *drawing* as the recital of a printed passage has as *reading* when proper phrasing and appreciation of the sense to be conveyed are neglected. Thus, the thorough memorising of forms, which is so necessary in direct brush drawing, renders this practice a most valuable training.

134. The Value of Memory Drawing.—Memory drawing may be made a valuable part of the child's education, and must not be considered a separate branch of study. The effort of memory is merely extended and applied to forms as a whole instead of in part. Its purpose may be compared with certain forms of literary composition such as the reproduction in writing of the substance of a passage read.

"Writing," says Bacon, "maketh an exact man," and this applies with equal force to Drawing, especially Memory Drawing. By memorising the proportions and shapes of things and studying the functions of their parts, the powers of observation and reasoning are sharpened. Further, the scholar's vocabulary of forms is gradually increased until he is able to represent objects once seen with comparative ease and express his ideas as readily with the pencil as the pen.

135. Methods of Training.—The exercises should be arranged in progressive order of difficulty and in varied form. They must be performed regularly from the earliest stage.

The style of drawing should be bold and rapid, rarely . occupying more than ten to fifteen minutes. For this reason the Freearm method is generally best suited for the purpose. The exercise may be conducted at the beginning or *occasionally* at the end of the drawing lesson. The more proficient scholars may employ their spare time in this way when their class exercise has been satisfactorily finished.

The children should not be restricted as to the mode of execution. They may be encouraged to indicate mass and light and shade in a simple manner. *Colour* as well as form may be indicated by means of crayons or brush if these materials are at hand.

136. Various Forms of Memory Drawing Lessons. 1st Form.—*Drawing an object which has been exhibited for a few minutes.* The object may be handled by the children if necessary. It is then put out of sight or covered if a particular position is desired for later reference. The children should be set to work without help or comment on the part of the teacher.

A glance round the class while the work is in progress should be sufficient to detect the drawings that show faulty observation or want of intelligence. Great accuracy of detail cannot be insisted upon. Note should be made of common errors. The object should be shown again and the children led to see their faults in drawing. These might be dealt with more fully with the objects and drawings in view at the following lesson. Defects are often more apparent to the pupil when the drawing is, examined again after an interval of time.

The power of visualising is difficult to attain. A most familiar form may be found elusive when an attempt is made to reproduce it from memory. The necessary concentration of mind is very limited in young children. The colour or tone of an object may obtrude itself on the mind so as to interfere with the observation of its form. Therefore in the early exercises the forms selected should be very simple in form, and, as far as possible, of a neutral tone. The use of a background of contrasting tone will be found helpful.

137. Directing the Observation.—Where the children's efforts have not been generally successful, the teacher may *occasionally* and previous to the second attempt *silently* direct their attention along certain lines of the object until they learn to seek essentials for themselves. Thus, if the object be a cricket bat, it might be suspended against the blackboard so as to be seen in elevation. The teacher would point to the proportions—his actions being imitated by the children—the extreme length and that of the handle and blade and the extreme breadth being compared. The slightly hollow curve of the handle and the curves of the shoulder and bottom of the blade would be traced next by the teacher and scholars in turn.

At a later stage, two analogous forms should be employed, the first to demonstrate various points, the second for the purpose of independent observation on the part of the children.

138. 2nd Form of Exercise.—*To reproduce from memory a form drawn at a previous lesson, and* (if the necessary elements of perspective have been studied) *from a different point of view.*

139. 3rd Form of Exercise.—*Drawing of an object studied out of school.* This form of memory drawing admits of infinite variety and is suitable for older scholars.

The choice of object may be left to the pupil or may be specified by the teacher. A fixed period is given for preparation, during which sketches may be submitted for the teacher's criticism or advice. The test should be done, of course, without reference to notes or sketches.

The following are suitable subjects for study :—Things seen in the home, schoolroom, playground, street, park, field, country, museum, on the sea, seashore, river, or railway; kitchen utensils, furniture, toys, and personal belongings (pocket-knife, top, rabbit-hutch, cage, etc.), garden implements, tools; house and shop fronts, gas or electric-light standards and lamps, iron and wooden gates, fire-alarm, vehicles; uniforms of soldier, policeman, fireman, etc., etc.

140. 4th Form of Exercise.—*Drawing from dictation a geometrical model or simple common object based on it with which the children are familiar.* Thus,

(*a*) Give the appearance of a large bowl
  (i) Placed horizontally about a foot from the ground,
  (ii) Inverted,
  (iii) Suspended horizontally about two feet above the children's eye-level.
A straw-hat lying horizontally; the same hung on a peg above the eye-level.

(*b*) Represent two flower-pots side by side, one upright, the other lying on its side.

(*c*) Represent an empty cigar-box as if placed on the desk in front of the one at which each scholar is seated, the lid being open in an upright position from the spectator and receding slightly towards the right.

(*d*) Represent an object in front of the class such as a wall map, room door, etc., in a different given position.

141. 5th Form of Exercise.—*Drawing ornamental or natural forms from memory ;* e.g. a design on the cover of a school reading-book, ornamental feature in or about the school, etc.

142. Drawing from Imagination.—The desire to express ideas by means of drawing is natural to most young children. They delight in " drawing something " in their own way despite their want of power, and are unconscious of the ludicrous effects that frequently characterise their efforts.

This form of recreative drawing is not so attractive to older scholars owing to the fact that they are more conscious of their lack of power of expression. The practice, however, may be continued with profit, since it affords a means of putting the formal teaching into practice and applying the knowledge gained by memory drawing. It also leads to independent study of forms for the purposes of illustration. It is an appropriate form of home practice.

Exercises.—*Young children* may be set to draw anything according to their fancy ; to illustrate the subject of a previous lesson, such as the horse, a plant, a common object ; a farmer, workman, or postman, in performance of their duties ; nursery rhymes, *e.g.* " Jack and Jill," " Old Mother Hubbard," etc. ; a fable, fairy tale, or Bible story ; subject of the reading lesson, school song or recitation ; games, *e.g.* playing with doll, hoop, etc. ; scenes in the school, playground, fields, street, or home. *Nature study,* including life and habits of domestic animals, cat, dog, etc.

Coloured chalks or crayons should be used, these being the most pleasing to young children.

Suitable exercises for older scholars are incidents and scenes described in reading, recitation, and history lessons.

Scenes and occupations in the street, market-place, field, farm, railway station, at the seaside, etc., *e.g.* a man delivering coal, milk, bread, etc., a road-sweeper, gardener, builder, farm labourer, blacksmith, carpenter at work, organ-grinder, blind beggar and dog, etc. *Deeds of heroism*—a boy saving another from drowning, a fireman carrying a child down an escape from a burning house.

CHAPTER XIII.

DRAWING AS A MEANS OF TEACHING.—SUGGESTIONS FOR STUDY.

Excellence is never granted to man, but as the reward of labour; a faculty of drawing, like that of playing upon a musical instrument, cannot be acquired but by an infinite number of acts.—SIR JOSHUA REYNOLDS.

143. Requirements for Students in Training Colleges.—The following is an extract from the prescribed course of study in Drawing.

" Acquisition of power to—

" (*a*) observe attentively, know accurately, and represent truthfully natural and artificial objects;

" (*b*) use the blackboard for class teaching;

" (*c*) draw from memory, knowledge, and imagination.

" (*a*) The chief aim should be the formation of habits of attentive observation, the acquisition of accurate knowledge of general form, organic and inorganic, and of the form and main characteristics of natural objects, and the power to express correctly the results of observation and knowledge.

" (*b*) For class teaching drawing on the blackboard should be rapidly and directly executed with a full appreciation and knowledge of the main characteristics of the subjects drawn, especially of their form and appearance; its chief aim and use in class is to enable the teacher to help the children to see, to think, to form clear ideas, and acquire accurate knowledge in all subjects of the School Curriculum, and to express their ideas by drawing as well as by words.

" (c) The teacher must therefore cultivate the power of retaining and expressing visual impressions; he must acquire knowledge of form and of the forms and characteristics of things, so as to be able to draw from memory and knowledge; and by constructive imagination to use this knowledge for instruction generally. The various subjects of the School Curriculum, e.g. Science, History, Geography, Nature Study, etc., will furnish suitable material for practice under these sections."

144. Acquirement of Knowledge of Forms of Common Things.—This is as necessary for the teacher as the possession of a fund of general information. Just as the latter essential is dependent on varied and well-digested reading rather than the mere cramming of facts, the knowledge and expression of form is dependent on frequent and patient study. No text-book can take the place of first-hand knowledge obtained by observation. The following hints, however, may help to show the student the lines on which he should work.

145. Method of Sketching.—Assuming the student can draw moderately well, he should aim at acquiring an easy and rapid style of sketching under varying conditions.

Elaborate preparations as for formal drawing should not be made. The habit should be cultivated of drawing in a standing position with a small, stiff sketch-book or block held in the left hand. A short, not too-finely pointed pencil should be held *inside* the hand so as to make a small angle with the paper.

Aim at Decision of Work.—Avoid the use of the rubber, or use it very rarely indeed. Sketching with a stylographic or fountain pen will be found a good corrective for indecision in work. A line should be "felt for," and when found, put in firmly so as to distinguish it from incorrect or working lines which may remain. Long, continuous lines may be represented by comparatively short, disconnected strokes. The mind must be concentrated mainly on the rapid translation of *form*—the character of the *line* is of secondary importance.

146. Main Principles of Drawing.—*Proportion.*
Faulty proportion is the most frequent cause of bad drawing. The method of early training in which too much reliance is placed on actual measurement rather than the
cultivation of the unaided *judgment* by sight is probably
largely accountable for this common weakness.
A number of short exercises should be performed, for a
few minutes each day, in recording without any mechanical
aid whatever the proportions of surrounding objects until
a proper degree of proficiency is obtained. Short strokes
may be set down to represent the various parts of an
object, *always beginning with whole form and proceeding
from the greater to the lesser parts.*
Balance or Symmetry of forms should be practised without the aid of lines of construction. These are necessary
occasionally, but the habit of using medial and horizontal
lines for the simplest balanced form should be discontinued.
Perspective.—The *rules* are few and simple, and their
application will aid the student up to a certain point.
Thus, in drawing a *box* he may remember that the parallel
edges which recede must be represented by converging
lines. But the actual degree of recedence or convergence
of lines and of the foreshortening of plane surfaces can
be appreciated by the majority of students only after pro-
longed study. In the case of the less regular curves,
especially such as occur in natural forms, the difficulties
are vastly increased.

147. Cultivation of the Power of Observation.—
The student is recommended to practise according to the
method already described. This practice may not carry
him far enough for his purpose, he will need to subject
himself to a strenuous course of observation exercises in
order to cultivate what may be termed the " perspective
eye." No special time need be assigned for this practice.
Ample opportunities occur every day and everywhere—in
the home, while walking, waiting for the train, travelling,
etc. No actual drawing need be performed, merely study
the *appearance* of things with the set purpose of seeing
them projected on to an imaginary vertical plane.

Thus, the front view is obtained of a flight of stairs. First notice the proportions—the apparent height of the whole flight compared with the greatest width and the latter with the height of the bannister; next, the gradual diminution of the width and depth of the horizontal surfaces of the "treads" as seen from below, the appearance of the edges of the carpet, of the stair rods, the vertical lines of the handrail, etc. Then notice the altered appearance of the staircase as seen anglewise.

Observe the appearance of similar objects according to the view presented by each, such as a group of boats lying on the water at different angles. Note the subtle curves of their outlines and compare with those lying on the beach.

148. The Application of Model Drawing.—Proficiency in drawing from the geometrical models may be made of great practical value, providing an analogy be drawn wherever possible between them and the object under observation. Thus, the treatment of the outlines of a building with sloping roof may be compared with that of the square prism surmounted by the triangular prism, or a square tower and steeple may be based on the lines of a square prism surmounted by a square pyramid.

149. The Mirror as an Aid to the Study of Form.— The method of tracing the contour of an object on a transparent glass plane has been described (Art. 89). A mirror also will be found useful for the purpose. It should be set up vertically at right angles to the direction of sight and the object suspended or placed in front of it. The reflection will show a reverse but perfect perspective view. An imaginary or actual line may be traced over the lines of the reflection and so assist the student in the appreciation of the appearance of forms. The drawings of the pipe (p. 93) might have been obtained in this manner.

A mirror will also be of great value in demonstrating the appearance of the foreshortening of parts of the body such as the hand, arm, etc. The reflection of oneself in a cheval glass will serve to study the proportions of the body —length of head, trunk, limbs—various poses, or the appearance of articles of clothing or drapery.

150. Preparation for Memory Drawing.—A thick sketch-book made of good cartridge paper is best for careful drawings of objects or sketches suitable for illustration of lessons. To facilitate future reference and study, it may be indexed and divided into sections; thus:—

1. *Artificial Forms*—singly and in groups—such as: (*a*) common domestic utensils, furniture, dress; (*b*) *Architectural Forms*; *e.g.* a cottage, church, or other building, windmill, bridge, well, etc. Ornamental forms and distinctive features of various styles of architecture, *e.g.* comparative sketches of a Norman and Early English arch, *or*

2. *Objects Specially Suitable for Illustration of Lessons:*—

(*a*) *History.*—Dress, armour, implements of war of various periods; illustrations for a lesson, such as the Early Britons (coracles, huts, etc.), the Crusades.

(*b*) *Geography*—illustrations for physical geography.

(*c*) *Literature*, including historical novels, such as "Ivanhoe."

(*d*) *Science and Observation Lessons.*—Experiments, apparatus, *Inventions*: comparative drawings of early and modern forms, *e.g.* the steam-engine. *Recent inventions*: parts of a gramaphone, telephone, a flying machine.

(*e*) *Nature Study.*—Comparative drawings of the most common plants, flowers, cereals, fruits, vegetables, trees; fish, bird, and insect life.

Animal Forms.—Types of common domestic and wild animals: horse, cow, sheep, dog, cat; elephant, camel; lion, tiger, etc.

The Human Form.—Main proportions and parts of the body.

Objects suggestive of the various seasons, e.g. *Spring :* the swallow, lambs, etc., buttercups, daisies, bud forms, etc.; *Summer :* corn, poppies, etc.; *Autumn :* fruit; *Winter :* bare trees, their characteristic forms; holly, mistletoe; the robin, snow-man, skates, etc.

Scenes and Natural Phenomena.—Mountains, valleys, lakes; clouds, sunset, etc.

151. Hints on Outdoor Sketching.—The object or scene to be sketched should be carefully selected. Some time should be given to getting the best pictorial view, and the drawing should be properly placed on the page. The rules of composition should be kept in mind and brought into use as occasion offers.

The sketch (Fig. 133) shows how the chief of these rules can be applied. In the foreground is a laden barge, which is the chief object in the picture; this is moored to some piles by the river bank, which, with the exception of the

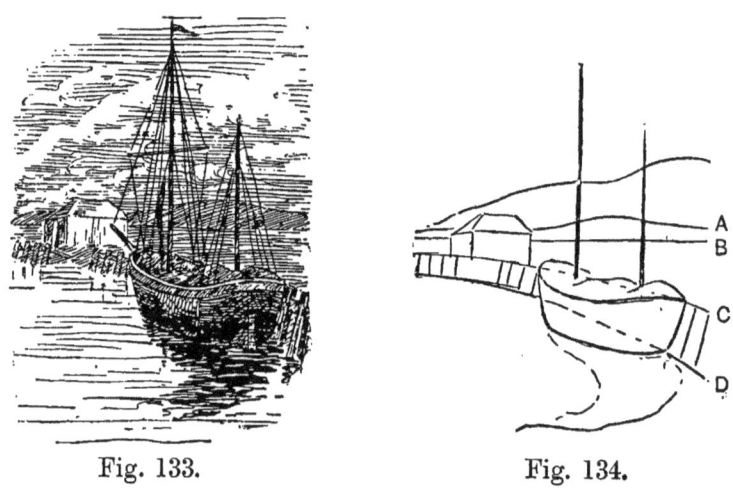

Fig. 133.   Fig. 134.

slope to the water, is level and monotonous. The piles are repeated further down the bank in groups of four. The repetition of the piles and the radiating curves of the bank give the effect of distance. The outline of the hills in the distance forms a great curve radiating towards the left, and the straight horizon line radiating to the same point makes a useful contrast. The chief lines of composition, then, are the four radiating lines A, B, C, D (Fig. 134). The orderly arrangement of the clouds and of the posts-in the water give a continuity to the scene, and the upright masts of the vessel present the necessary contrast to the general horizontal effect of the picture. Thus the chief principles of Balance, Radiation, Continuity, Repetition, and Contrast are all present.

An endeavour should be made, in the first place, to use as few lines as possible. This will train the student to select the essential outlines, and is in itself a valuable training.

The representation of foliage (Fig. 135) gives some trouble at first, but if the main outlines are correctly drawn and the various *masses* of leaves added, the effect of light and shade can easily be produced as shown in

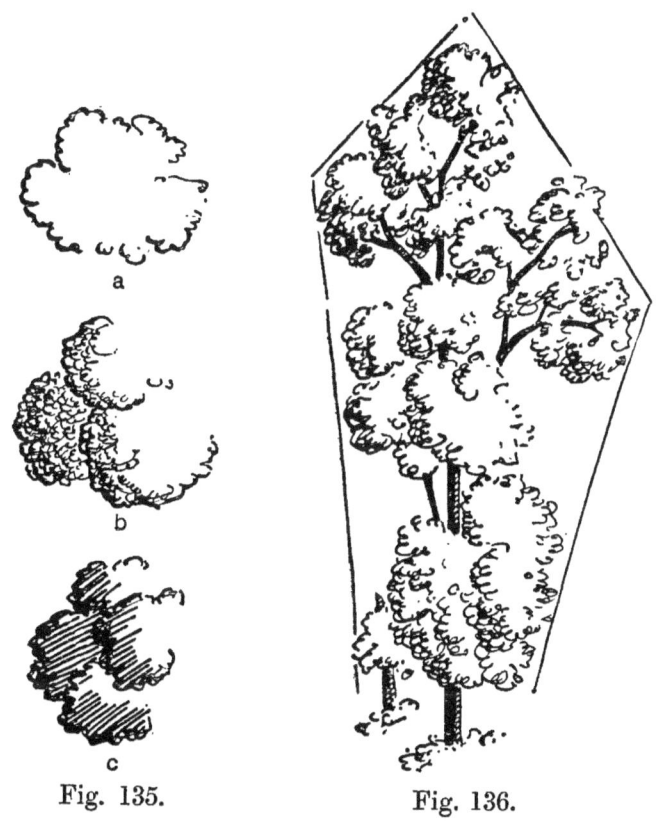

Fig. 135.   Fig. 136.

Figs. 135, 136 and 138. The careful drawing of trunk and branches where visible is of course essential to truthful representation. Distance may be shown by using lighter lines.

Water may be represented when calm by horizontal lines, as in Fig. 137; when disturbed by wavy lines, as in Fig. 139. The light and shade on the waves should be noted, and the effect of distance obtained by gradual decrease in size.

The outlines of various types of clouds should be studied and sketched from nature, the sky being a most important part of every landscape.

152. Drawing from Diagrams and Pictures.—Many objects necessary for the purposes of illustration may be found in local museums. Recourse must be had, sometimes, to pictures of them. Even professional artists find

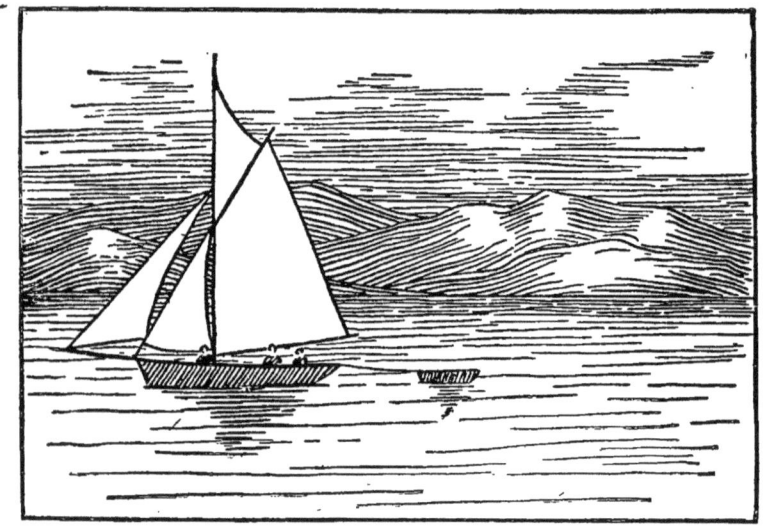

Fig. 137.

this necessary at times. Copying of pictures may be made a valuable and instructive exercise if done intelligently. Should an illustration be required of an object that is not accessible, various pictures giving different views of the same form should be studied for the purpose of selecting essential lines of structure. The student should then endeavour to represent the object from a different point of view by the aid of his knowledge of the principles of perspective.

153. Rapid Visualising and Sketching.—Good practice can be obtained by sitting at a window overlooking a street, and preferably facing a turning.

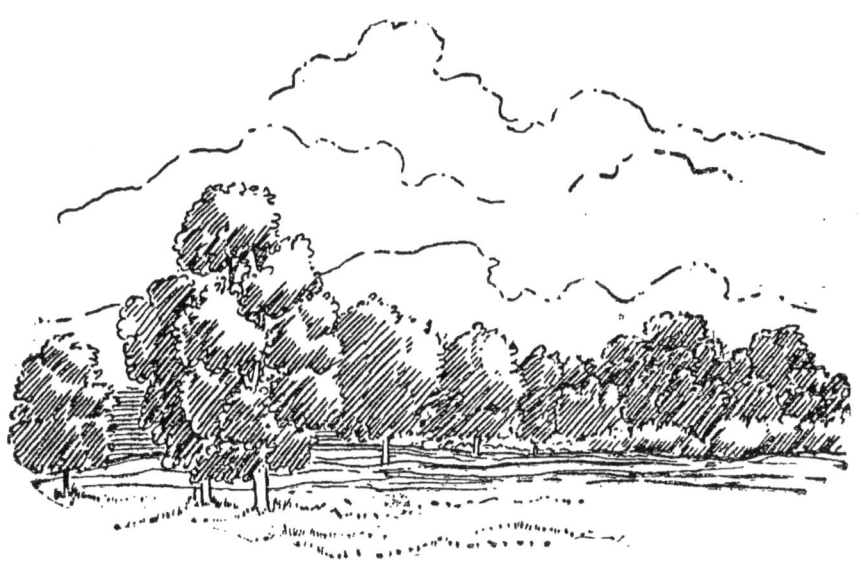

Fig. 138.
Method of sketching groups of trees.

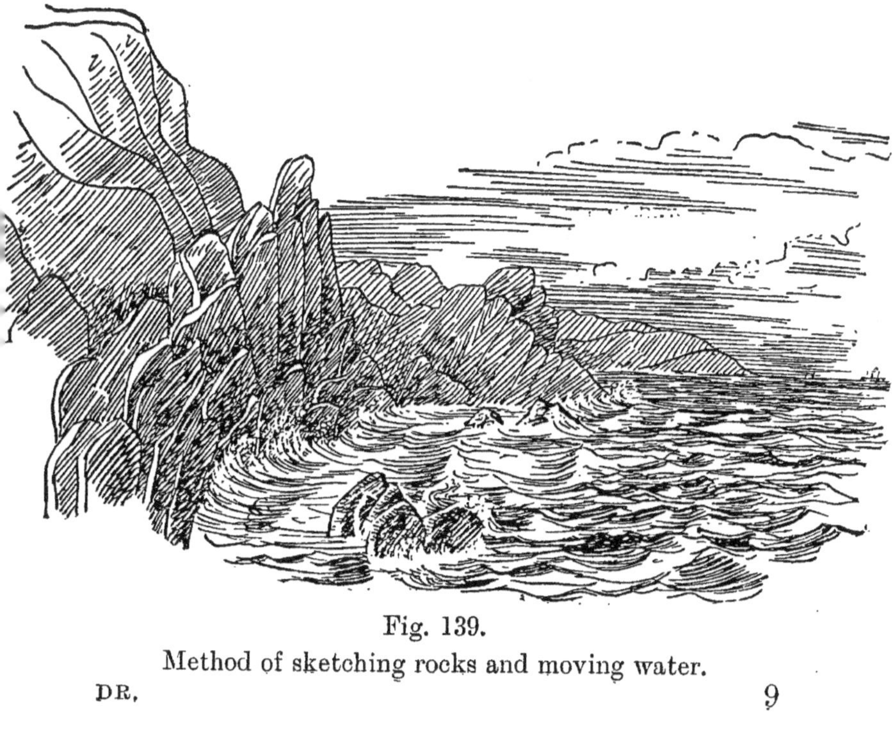

Fig. 139.
Method of sketching rocks and moving water.

Moving Objects.—A man pushing a truck along, a child bowling a hoop, a dog running, all suggest studies. Fix the eyes intently in order to take in the general appearance, pose, and essential parts of the object or group. Close the eyes and test the impression made on the retina. Repeat the process and then attempt to set down the impression, omitting unimportant details and introducing suggestive and characteristic details.

154. Suggestion in Art.—The suppression of detail is a most important and necessary device in sketching from

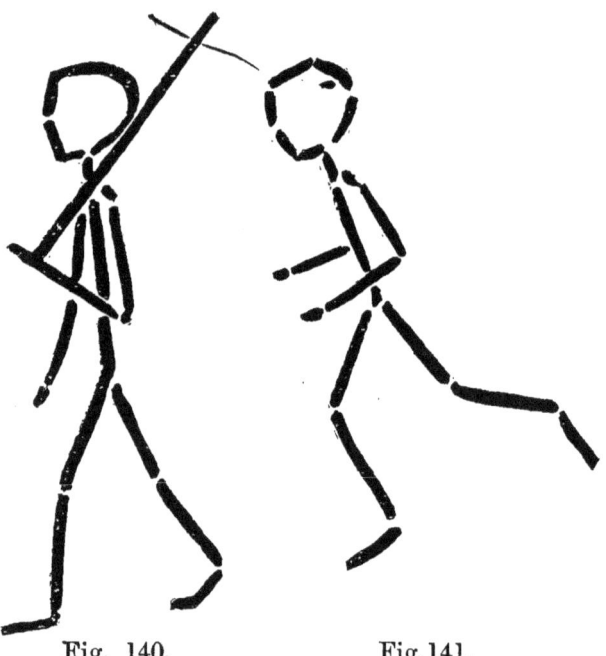

Fig. 140.   Fig.141.

life. Every stroke should be carefully considered with the view to its effectiveness or possible omission. Attention should be given first to the pose, which may be indicated in skeleton lines (Figs. 140 and 141), and next combined with *masses* showing the proportions (see sketch of boy fishing, Fig. 142).

Figs. 143   144 are illustrations of the effect obtained by comparative size and positions of objects in a picture,

In the first, the balloon is suggested by the basket and ropes. In mind we are with the occupant of the basket. The other forms are quite small in comparison. In the second illustration there is the suggestion of great height combined

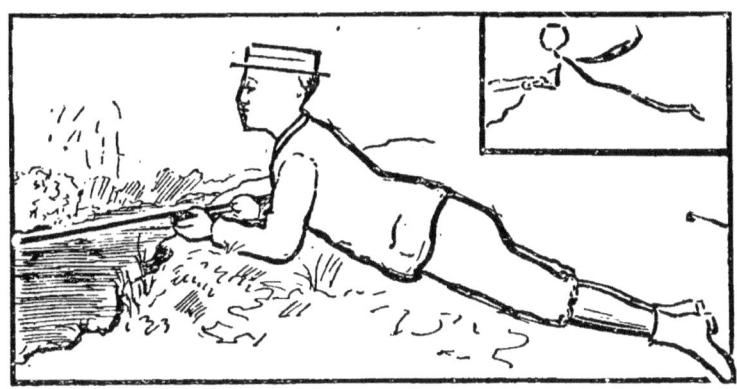

Fig. 142.

with distance of the balloons from each other. We cannot see the expression on the faces of the spectators, but by their *attitudes* we should expect one to show *wonder* and the other mere *interest*. Thus the mind readily supplies details wanting in a picture, or where they cannot be distinguished in actual scenes.

155. Constructive Imagination.—The student having obtained some facility in drawing forms from memory should next attempt to combine them so as to produce a " picture." Such pictures probably will not be worthy of the designation in an artistic sense, but the student should take courage and persevere, with the knowledge that a teacher is not expected to undergo the training necessary for an artist. His efforts may be very crude and exhibit anomalies in drawing, but, providing they appeal to the not too critical minds of children and convey the idea intended, they have fulfilled their purpose.

Simplicity of treatment should be aimed at. Much may be learnt in this respect by the study of methods employed by artists. Ample opportunities for self-education may be found in art galleries and exhibitions, cheap and well-illustrated literature, and even in the advertisements in magazines. Direct attention to line, form, light and shade, composition, and scheme of colour of the picture, the method by which effects of distance and projection are produced, and the treatment of particular forms, such as foliage, etc.

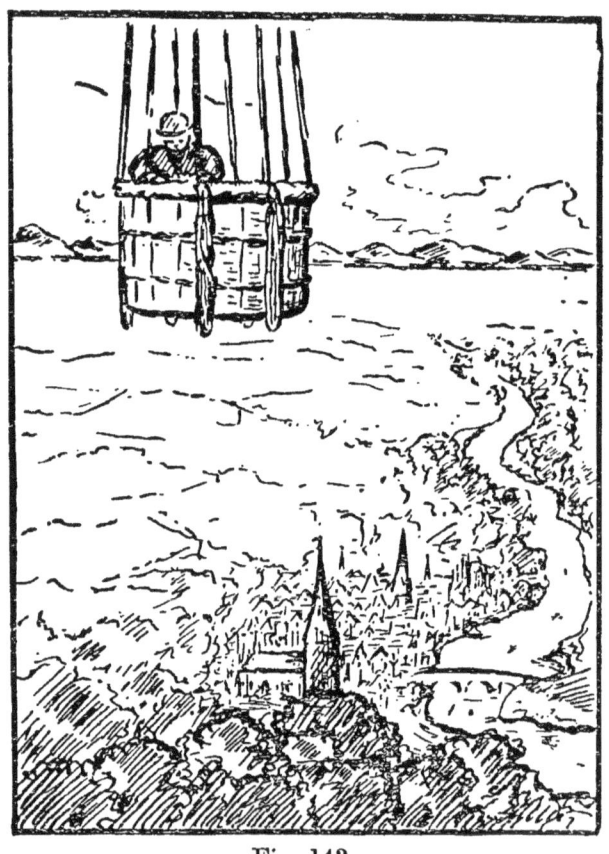

Fig. 143.

156. The Use of Various Media for Demonstration.—Drawing may be applied (1) for the purpose of illustration in connection with *any* lesson, (2) to demonstrate form or the method of expression incidental to the *drawing* lesson.

Drawing with chalk or tempera on the blackboard is the most generally useful method of illustration. Facility in the use of the blackboard is absolutely essential for successful teaching. Special training is necessary to master the difficulties peculiar to this mode of expression.

The teacher should be prepared also to execute drawings

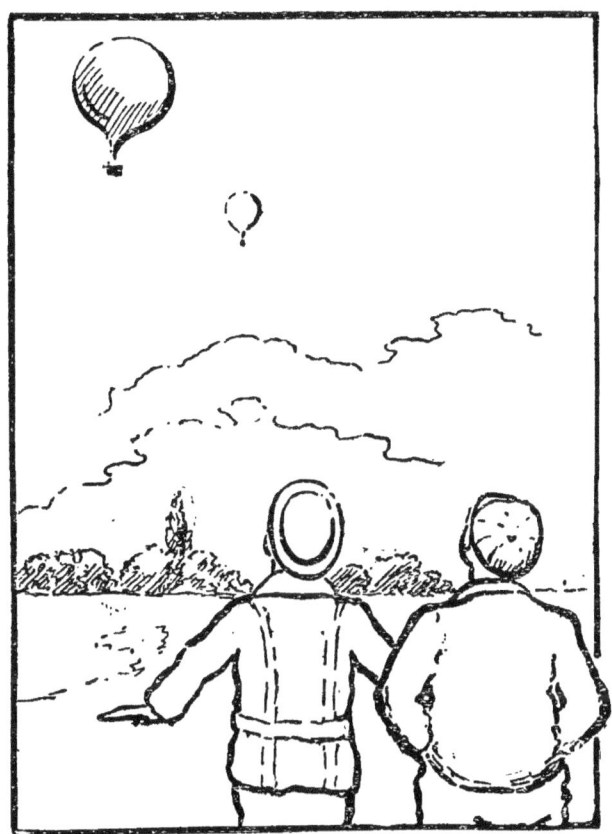

Fig. 144.

to a large scale in view of the class *in the drawing medium employed by the scholars.* This tends to sustain their interest, makes them keen to imitate, while the fact that the teacher is dealing with the same difficulties as themselves inspires the pupils with confidence.

157. Hints on Blackboard Drawing.—The body should be "square" to the blackboard and a fair distance from it. The right foot may be advanced slightly.

The drill movements described (Art. 21) should be practised regularly. The drawings must be clearly visible from a distance, therefore make the lines firm and broad and the drawings simple in character. Reduce all detail to a minimum. Flat tones may be represented occasionally by means of the broad of the chalk, but avoid elaborate shading. The execution should be rapid and direct. Plan the whole of the picture in mind so that each line may be set down on the board without hesitation. Drawings should be made from carefully prepared sketches or, preferably, from the memory of them. The principal masses may be lightly "blocked in." The lines of construction should be few and simple.

Variety of Line.—As progress is made, the student should endeavour to produce other than bold, uniform lines such as are suitable for mere diagrams. He should realise the capacity of the chalk for beautiful expression of line and introduce variety where this is likely to be effective. The character of forms, especially natural ones, may often be expressed in this way, such as the texture of animal coverings—fur, feathers, etc., rough or smooth bark of trees, angularity or roundness of objects. Compare the woolly appearance of the sheep with the sleekness of the body of the pig, the round smooth form of the infant with the vigorous, "square" lines of the man. All these peculiarities may be portrayed by means of variation in the enclosing lines of the drawing, by broadening, tapering, or breaking their continuity.

Perspective effects may be produced also by varying the thickness of lines. Thus, the near or projecting edges of rectangular objects should be represented by bolder lines than the more remote; the roundness of curved forms, such as the mouth of a circular vessel or the near edge of a foreshortened leaf, by broadening the nearer portion of the edges. This "expression" should be produced by varying the pressure on the chalk, not by "painting" the line.

CHAPTER XIV.

THE STUDY OF PICTURES.—VISITS TO PICTURE GALLERIES.

Nothing is of the least use to young people, but what interests them; and therefore, though it is of great importance to put nothing but good art into their possession, yet when they are passing through great houses or galleries, they should be allowed to look precisely at what pleases them.

RUSKIN.

158. Importance of the Study of Pictures.—An important development in elementary art teaching is the systematic study of pictures, especially great pictures. No education can be complete without some knowledge of the pictorial records bequeathed to us by the painters of the past. The Memorandum on the Teaching of Drawing, issued by the Scotch Education Department, contains the following paragraph:—

"The study and appreciative criticism of fine pictures and other examples of artistic expression, either in the original when such are available, or through good reproductions, can be made in competent hands the vehicle of an excellent training in art appreciation and the perception of beauty. A visit to an art gallery or museum under suitable guidance affords ideal opportunities for educational picture and sculpture study, and many a cultured art lover would be only too glad to give his services in such a cause. Similar educational visits should also be made to whatever interesting buildings, etc., are available, so that the children may learn to know and appreciate the various art and other treasures within their own domain."

Only good pictures should be used in the decoration of the school-room. Diagrams and maps are best rolled up, and only exhibited when required for lessons. The quality of the illustrations in Geography, History, and Nature Study books should be carefully considered when new books are ordered.

159. Suggestions for Elementary Lessons in Picture Study.

Talks about Artists and their Pictures.—A single, large picture would serve as illustration for such a lesson. The pupils would be interested in finding out the full meaning of the picture and in hearing something about the artist. The children should be allowed to bring pictures of their own, and the teacher may use these for lessons. Reproductions of famous pictures are easily obtainable now.

Lessons on Composition.—The pupils may be led—

    i. To discover the title of the picture.

    ii. To find out the meaning and use of details.

    iii. To notice the dress and action of the figures.

    iv. To look at the background, sky, or setting of the picture.

    v. To study the colours used and their relations.

    vi. To find out the dark and light parts.

Essay Writing.—The pupils are set to describe a picture in their own words. The essays are criticised by the class and teacher.

160. The Value of Picture Study.—The study of great pictures is a valuable part of education for the following reasons:—

    1. *It is an aid to the study of history.* The incidents and portraits recorded at the time by pictorial art help us to understand more exactly the nature of the scenes and the character of the people we read about in our history books.

    2. *It is an aid to the study of geography.* The landscape of Tuscany, the canals of Venice, the gardens of France,

and the scenery of Holland can easily be imagined if we look at the right pictures in the National Gallery.

3. *It is an aid to Nature study.* The beauties of the sky and sea and the colours of foliage under different aspects of light will be more appreciated after a glance through the artist's spectacles.

4. *It trains the aesthetic feeling.* The standard of taste and refinement in artistic matters is raised by a study of the great masters.

5. *It gives patterns of expression.* Our ability to express our ideas is limited, but may be increased by studying the methods employed by artists. Admiration and delight in the skill and patience exhibited in this way will increase our own power. Our imagination is stimulated.

6. *It increases our knowledge of human nature.* We must study other people who live under different conditions and with different ideals if we wish to understand some great pictures. This will give us wider views and a greater interest in life.

7. *It leads us to study the principles of art*, and consequently to take a deeper interest in literature, music, and architecture. The unity necessary in the composition of a work of art helps us to understand the necessity for consistency with a purpose in our lives. Moral lessons may be brought home to us, as in music and literature.

161. The Study of Old Masters.—To understand and appreciate fully a picture by the old masters it is necessary to study the following points :—

1. *Its school, period, and date.* Each school possesses certain characteristic features, either in composition, technique, or subject—*e.g.* the Italian School is represented chiefly by religious and mythological works, designed in the first place to decorate churches and other important buildings.

2. *The history of the town, province, or country concerned.* To understand Venetian art we must read the story of its great and prosperous period, when it was the chief port in the South of Europe.

3. *The life and ideals of the people at the time*, especially of the upper classes, who were the patrons of the Arts. The state of French society just previous to the Revolution is reflected in the art of Watteau, Boucher, etc.

4. *The nature of the country from a geographical point of view.* The flat, uninteresting surface of Holland is

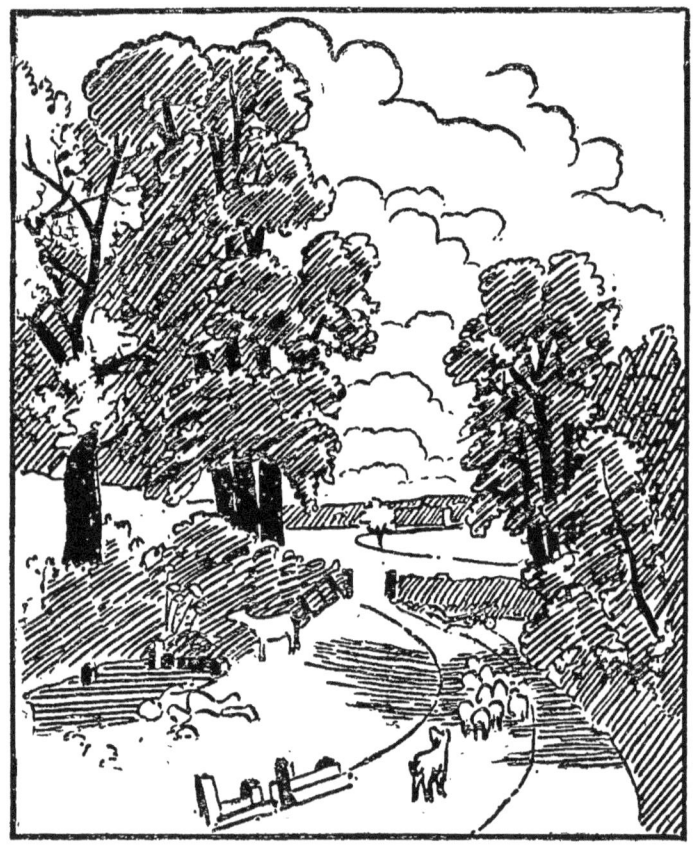

Fig. 145.

accountable to a certain extent for the unromantic-nature of Dutch art.

5. *The technique of painting.* The difficulties of the early painters in finding materials and methods of manipulating them should be understood. Tempera, mosaic, and oil-colour methods of painting need explanation.

6. *The life and personality of the painter*—his aims and ideals.

162. The Composition of a Picture.—We will take the well-known landscape picture in the National Gallery, Constable's " Cornfield," and analyse it according to the laws of beauty mentioned in drawing from nature (p. 48) and in drawing from ornament (Chap. XI.).

Balance.—The picture is well balanced. A mass of trees on either side with a horizontal stretch of country between was a favourite form of composition employed by Claude, the first landscape artist, and Turner, his successor. The chief lines may be represented thus (Fig. 146) :—

Compare the pictures on page 143 (Figs. 147 and 148).

Claude's landscape is a purely formal composition.

Turner's picture is transitional. It is no doubt drawn from nature, but shows Claude's influence in arrangement. The trees are too tall and the foreground raised.

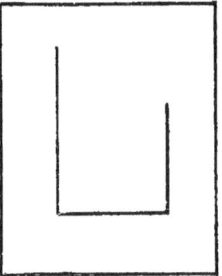

Fig. 146.

Constable's "Cornfield" is true to nature both with regard to composition and details.

Radiation.—Important lines radiate from the gateway, the sides of the pathway, and hedges. The two groups of trees are formed by the radiating trunks and its main branches radiate to their respective trunks.

Repetition.—The leaves of the trees mass themselves together in graceful forms ; these forms repeat themselves, and so build up the tree. The group of trees on the left is a repetition of the group on the right. The wayside flowers occur in groups, and so do the waving grass and ears of corn. The tree in the centre of the cornfield is like an echo of the near trees, which are echoed again in the far distance. The procession of sheep controlled by the shepherd's dog helps to give a pleasant *Rhythm* to the picture. The clouds, too, are crossing the sky in a similar procession.

Curvature.—Notice the curves of the roadway, the line dividing the fields in the distance, and the lines of the tree-trunks. The curves of the withered branch speak of its past beauty and help us to understand the loveliness of the clothed branches. The curves enclosing the masses of foliage are similar to those outlining the clouds.

Contrast.—The horizontal field of corn makes a pleasing contrast to the tall elms; the straight-lined timbers propping up the bank are in direct opposition to the rounded forms of the sheep. The light and shade in this picture is well distributed. Notice the shadow of the trees across the road and the play of light on the backs of the sheep. The withered tree serves to emphasise the beauty of the living. The colours are well arranged and shown to perfection by suitable contrast.

Other points in the picture noticed by pupils and extracted from their essays are as follows :—

" The eye takes in the whole of the scene at once. Nothing occurs to distract the attention from the main subject of the picture. Everything is in perfect harmony and each detail tends to enhance the chief idea—that of perfect repose in nature."

" The open gate, however, marks the true artist. Imagine that gate to be shut, and the whole effect of the picture is altered—the foreground becomes the principal feature and the cornfield merely subsidiary."

" The artist has shown great talent in his representation of the sky. He has fixed the eye-level below the middle of the picture, so that a large space is filled with a cloudy sky. The clouds are banked up one above another in great masses, as one may so frequently see them in summer."

" We see the sun is shining by the gleam of light through the trees."

" The curve of the shadows shows the slope of the bank."

" The trees form a frame to the rest of the picture."

To summarise, we might say that this picture is beautiful because it exhibits truth to nature in drawing, pleasing arrangement of masses and colour, and wonderful skill in the representation of English daylight and English rural scenery.

163. Preparation for Visiting a Picture Gallery.—
It is advisable for the teacher to visit the Gallery some
time previously, to decide which pictures his class shall
specially study. He may select the work of one artist,
and in this case he will give his pupils a short biography
with an account of the pictures available. These lessons
should be illustrated by a few good reproductions of the
artist's work. The teacher may, however, prefer to deal
with a group of artists and his lesson may be on a certain
School or he may like to compare the merits of several
Schools. With regard to modern pictures, it is better to
select a few representative specimens for careful study.

The number of pupils actually visiting the Gallery
should be limited to twenty. Each should be provided
with a list of pictures he is specially recommended to see,
with perhaps a few notes in description. On the paper he
should note any other pictures which he specially admires.
The pupils should be warned beforehand that some
pictures require a special view point; a near view is
not usually the best. The beauty and reality of details
are often more clearly seen by looking through a tube
(which can be made with the notepaper), and so shutting
out the straight-lined frame of the picture; the art of
light and shade becomes more evident when seen in
this way.

164. Specimen Notes of a Lesson.

Turner and his Pictures.

Introduction.—Joseph Mallord William Turner was the
greatest English landscape artist. He bequeathed 19,000
pictures and sketches to the nation. Some of these are
exhibited in the National Gallery, the greater number are
placed in the Tate Gallery, while others are arranged in
sets and lent to various provincial exhibitions. Many of
Turner's pictures, especially his large oil paintings, are not
understood and appreciated as they should be, but there
are many smaller water-colour drawings whose exquisite
beauty is felt by all.

Brief Story of his Life.—Turner was born in 1775 in Maiden Lane, Covent Garden. He showed talent when very young, and became a pupil of the Royal Academy School when 14 years of age. Sir Joshua Reynolds was one of his tutors. He was a great traveller and after thoroughly touring his native country he visited France, Germany, Italy, and Switzerland. He led a solitary and rather unhappy life, hoarded his money, and lived in a very frugal manner. He was a constant exhibitor at the Royal Academy, but it was only on "varnishing days," just before the Academy opened, that he was seen by his fellow Academicians. During the latter part of his life he was unable adequately to express his ideas, and the pictures produced at this time are difficult to comprehend. Some time before his death he disappeared, but was discovered leading an unhappy and lonely life in a cottage at Chelsea. He died at the age of 76. He left £20,000 to the Royal Academy and £1,000 for his monument in St. Paul's Cathedral.

His Art.—The art of Turner was not properly recognised during his lifetime. John Ruskin became interested in his pictures, and was led to write the five volumes of *Modern Painters* in defence of Turner. In these books he records his investigations into the beauties of nature and the history of art. He shows the "orderliness" of clouds, mountains, and trees, and proves conclusively that the majority of Turner's work is full of truth and beauty most skilfully expressed.

Turner's earlier pictures are composed in the rather formal manner of Claude, the French landscape artist, but they show an advance in realistic treatment. Compare the composition of Claude's "Landscape" (Fig. 147) and Turner's "Crossing the Brook" (Fig. 148), and for further advance in this style of composition see the picture by Constable described on p. 139.

Turner published a series of drawings of representative landscape, which he named the "Liber Studiorum," after the example of Claude, who published a similar work entitled "Liber Veritatis." The originals of many of these drawings are in the Tate Gallery. They are very fine models of landscape composition, and are worthy of much close study.

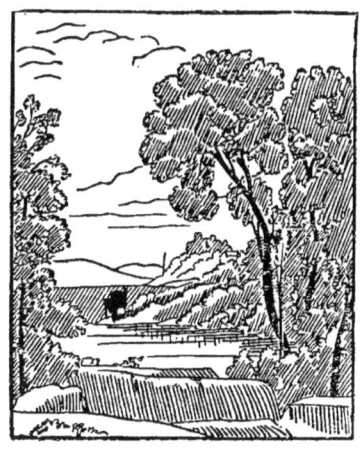

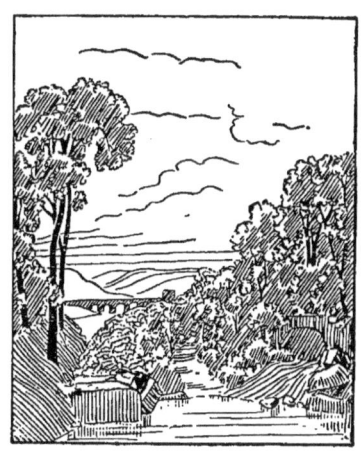

Claude.

Fig. 147.

Turner.

Fig. 148.

A few of Turner's Oil Pictures exhibited at the Tate Gallery :—

" *Crossing the Brook.*"—Study the composition. Note the wonderful sense of limitless space in the sky.

" *Bay of Baiæ.*"—Note the gradation of tone and how it helps to give immense distance.

" *Petworth Park* " and " *Chichester Canal.*"—Radiation is clearly the chief feature in the composition.

" *Ulysses deriding Polyphemus.*"—Notice the wonderful sky effect caused by the sunrise. "The most gorgeous piece of colour ever put upon canvas " is a critic's description. Tell the story of Ulysses. Note the giant on the mountains, the sea nymphs guiding the vessel, the fire in the cave, and Apollo with his horses outlined on the horizon.

" *Rain, Steam, and Speed.*"—This is an example of Turner's impressionist work and gives a fine representation of one of the earlier Great Western trains crossing a high bridge in a gale. Notice the little rabbit running from danger.

"*The Fighting Temeraire.*"—This is a sunset picture.
Notice the tall, ghost-like warship in contrast to the dark,
noisy tug. The water reflection is marvellously real. This
picture was one of Turner's last great works, and is typical
of his own decline.

A Visit to the Wallace Collection.

Let us suppose that the object of such a visit is to study
and compare certain representative pictures of the French,
Dutch, and English Schools. A lesson previously given
and illustrated by reproductions of some of the pictures
would greatly enhance its value. The following notes will
suggest suitable information.

165. History of the Collection.—The pictures and
objects of art were collected in Paris by the third and fourth
Marquesses of Hertford. The fourth Marquess bequeathed
the Collection to his lifelong friend, Sir Richard Wallace,
who had helped considerably in collecting the same. The
Collection was brought to London for safety at the time of
the disturbances following the Franco-Prussian War. The
pictures were exhibited in Bethnal Green Museum in 1872-5.
Sir Richard bequeathed the Collection to Lady Wallace,
who in turn carried out her husband's wish and gave the
whole to the British nation in 1897.

**166. French School of Seventeenth and Eighteenth
Centuries.**—This was the period in the history of France
which led up to the Revolution. There were two classes—
the minority, who possessed all the wealth and power, who
lived in idleness and luxury; and the poor, who were down-
trodden and badly governed. The Court and upper classes
employed the great painters of the time to paint pictures
of their idle dreams. These usually took the form of
picnics in beautiful gardens, surrounded by fountains,
statues, flowers and fruit. Here the lords and ladies were
represented in beautiful dresses amusing themselves by
music and dancing.

167. Chief Painters.—French School : Watteau, with his pupils **Lancret** and **Pater.** Painters of picnic scenes above described. Watteau's work is remarkable for the grace and delicacy of the figure drawing and the harmony of subdued colours. His grouping of figures is always worthy of study. (34 pictures.)

Boucher. His work is noteworthy for decorative composition. The harmony of bright colours is a special feature. (21 pictures.)

Madame Le Brun and **Nattier.** Portrait painters. Notice the peculiar colour of the cheeks and the custom of representing ladies of fashion as goddesses.

Greuze. A painter of graceful young girls. These pictures are supposed to represent the ideal of girlish beauty and innocence, but many show much unreal sentimentality and affectation. Compare with Sir Joshua Reynolds' truthful portrait of "Miss Bowles and her dog."

168. Dutch School : Rembrandt. Great portrait painter. Chief characteristics of his works are truth and realism in portraiture effected chiefly by a masterly understanding of light and shade. (10 pictures.) Study carefully :—

> " *The Unmerciful Servant.*"
> " *Jan Pellicorne and his son.*"
> " *Wife of Jan Pellicorne and daughter.*"

Notice specially the gradation of tone in the dark shadows. As we can distinguish objects in a dark room when we become accustomed to the small amount of light, so we can see more and more in Rembrandt's shadows.

Franz Hals. " *The Laughing Cavalier.*" As a portrait of vigorous manhood this picture has never been excelled. Note the marvellous representation of embroidery. "The twinkle in the eye," as seen in this picture, is characteristic of this artist's work.

169. English School: Sir Joshua Reynolds. The greatest of English portrait painters. (5 pictures.)
" *Nellie O'Brien.*" Note how the face is illumined by reflected light.

DR. 10

"The Strawberry Girl." ⎫ Examples of masterly
"Miss Bowles and her dog." ⎬ portraiture of children.
"Mrs. Carnac."

Reynolds.   *"Mrs. Robinson as Perdita."* ⎫ Compare
Romney.   *"Mrs. Robinson as Perdita."* ⎬ these.
Gainsborough. *"Mrs. Robinson as Perdita."* ⎭
 "Miss Haverfield."

Turner.   Four beautiful water-colour sketches :—
 "Woodcock Shooting."
 "Scarborough."
 "Grouse Shooting."
 "Mowbray Lodge."

170. Notes of Lessons on some Characteristics of the Chief Schools of Painting.—These lessons are intended to give a general view of the History of Painting. They should be given previously to the actual visits to the Galleries. A map of Europe showing the areas of the chief Schools with the principal art centres will be necessary (see Fig. 149), and the lessons should be illustrated by reproductions of the pictures.

The Art History of Europe is strongly bound up in her political and geographical records, and some knowledge of these will greatly assist in making the lessons interesting and instructive. The chronology of the works selected for study can be tabulated and explained (see Fig. 150). The comparative youth of the English School is here clearly shown and contemporary painters can easily be associated.

The table on page 148 suggests typical pictures by painters of the chief Schools. They are specially selected for study, not only because they display the characteristic features of the Old Masters, but because they give some idea of the work of the various Schools.

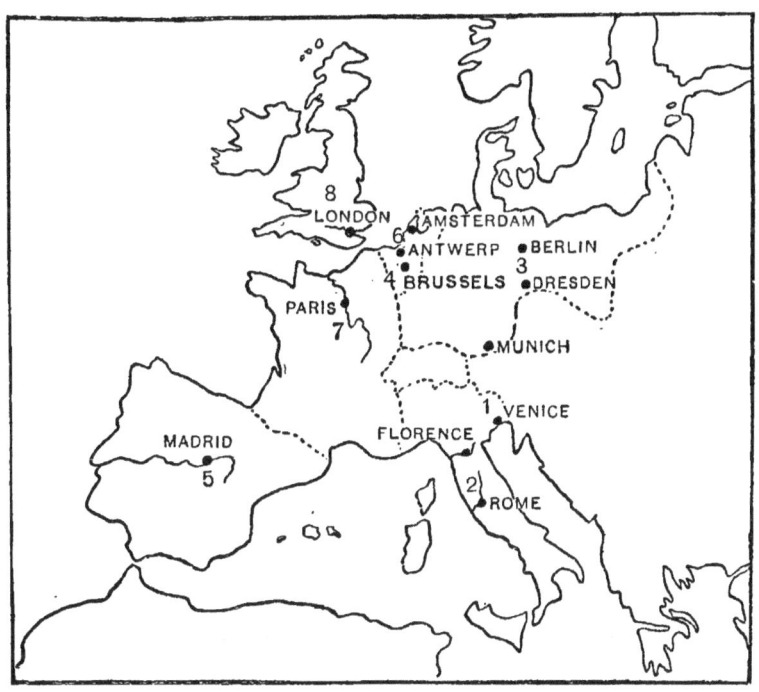

Fig. 149.

	School	Representative Painters	15th Century	16th Century	17th Century	18th Century	19th Century
1	Venetian — Italian	Titian	1477-1576				
2	Umbrian — Italian	Raphael	1485-1521				
3	German	Holbein	1497-1543				
4	Flemish	Rubens		1577-1640			
		Van Dyck		1599-1641			
5	Spanish	Velasquez		1599-1660			
		Murillo		1618-1682			
6	Dutch	Rembrandt		1607-1669			
7	French	Claude		1600-1682			
8	English	Reynolds			1723-1792		
		Turner				1775-1851	

Fig. 150.

Artist.	Pictures to Study. (National Gallery.)	Characteristic Features.
Titian	Bacchus and Ariadne	Splendid colour scheme. Representation of strong movement. Harmonious composition, especially of figures and background.
Raphael	The Ansidei Madonna The Vision of a Knight	Composition by symmetrical balance. Decorative pattern. Ideal representation of intellectual beauty.
Holbein	The Ambassadors Duchess of Milan	Truth in drawing. Marvellous detail. Delineation of character.
Rubens	The Judgment of Paris	Brilliant colour harmony. Representation of full, joyous, luxurious life.
Van Dyck	Portrait of Van der Gheest	Masterly representation of character in portraiture. Refined beauty and dignity of style.
Velasquez	Philip IV. of Spain Admiral Pulido Pareja	Truth in form, colour, light and shade. Natural and dignified pose of figures.
Murillo	The Holy Family A Spanish Peasant Boy	Expression of religious feeling. Fine composition. Representation of beggar boys in act of eating.
Rembrandt	His own Portrait Portrait of an Old Lady	Realism. Remarkable study of light and shade. Truthful portraiture. Wonderful drawing of personal ornaments.
Claude	Embarkation of the Queen of Sheba The Mill, or The Marriage of Isaac and Rebecca	Formal composition. Good representation of sunshine. Weak arrangement of figures.
Reynolds	Age of Innocence Lord Heathfield	Study of childhood. Representation of grace and beauty in portraiture.
Turner	Dido building Carthage	Good landscape composition. Representation of bright sunlight effects. Gorgeous colouring. Imaginative power.

CHAPTER XV.

THE CONSTRUCTION OF DRAWING SCHEMES.

171. Unity of Purpose should be the main consideration in devising any scheme of work. Even in the Lower School, where the ultimate aim of the scheme as a whole cannot be realised and the child is occupied mainly with discovering and developing his powers of expression along varied and pleasant lines, the Syllabus should show continuity of study with careful grading of exercises.

In the Middle School the purpose of the scheme should be made clear, whether it is to have an *industrial* or *aesthetic* tendency, while in the Upper School the aim should be developed further by increased specialisation.

172. Influences Affecting the Construction of a Scheme.—Many factors likely to influence the extent and direction of the teaching must be taken into account; thus:—

(*a*) *The Conditions and Needs of the Locality.*—In a manufacturing district special attention should be devoted to mechanical and industrial drawing, including design, etc., while in a country district special facilities may be found for the study of natural forms.

(*b*) *The Character of the General Instruction* must be taken into account with the view to the *correlation of work*. Such subjects as Nature study, manual training (woodwork, metalwork, etc.), and clay modelling should largely influence the course of drawing.

(c) *Equipment of the School—Furniture and Drawing Materials.*—Some schools are better equipped than others for teaching particular subjects, such as object and light and shade drawing. Some have set apart a specially appointed class-room for drawing, with ample floor-space, proper seating accommodation and lighting arrangements, while others are greatly deficient in these respects.

(d) *The Strength of the Staff and its Capacity for Teaching Drawing.*—In small schools, where a teacher has charge of more than one class, the stages must be comparatively few. A more ambitious scheme can be carried out where a drawing instructor is employed, or where a class teacher specially interested and qualified for the purpose can devote his energies to the whole or the greater part of the drawing instruction. The *interchange of teachers* according to their fitness for teaching a particular subject or stage is highly desirable.

(e) *Special Organisation of the School.*—The *grading* of children according to their capacity for drawing is very advantageous and leads to more rapid progress.

The *size* of classes is also an important factor. More individual attention is needed for advanced studies such as are carried out in Higher Grade and Higher Elementary Schools. Except for mechanical drawing, the teacher should not be responsible for more than twenty scholars at a time. Larger classes should be graded and divided into sections.

(f) *Amount of Time and Duration of Lessons.*—At least two hours a week should be devoted to the subject. In the upper classes this should be exclusive of mechanical drawing. The lessons should range from 30 to 40 minutes in the lower classes to 1 hour in the upper classes. For advanced work such as that of the upper forms of Higher Grade Schools the lesson may extend to $1\frac{1}{2}$ hours. One long lesson here will usually be more effective than two short ones.

Every exercise should be completed, as far as possible in one lesson, but advanced studies may occcasionally be extended with advantage over two or more lessons.

173. Summary of Subjects Suitable for Drawing Schemes.—Owing to varying conditions that prevail in different schools, as described above, it is impossible to prescribe schemes that would be suitable in every case. The following synopsis of most of the forms of drawing likely to be of use in drawing up a scheme is offered as a basis for *selection*. The subjects in some cases are marked off in stages, generally corresponding with the standards (see Preface), but these stages, as well as the subjects, must be selected to meet individual requirements. Detailed instructions and illustrations will be found in the body of the work.

SUBJECT.	STAGE.	APPLICATION.—NATURE OF EXERCISES, ETC.
1. DRAWING IN SAND.	Babies.	Simple objects and natural forms, with Memory and Imaginative Drawing.
2. DRAWING ON SLATES.	Infant Classes.	Ditto.
3. FREEARM DRAWING, including— (a) *Mass Drawing.* (b) *Mass Filling.*	Throughout the School.	On blackboards, millboards ; brown, tinted, or white paper. In charcoal, chalk, crayon, or pencil. Applied to Object and Model or Nature Drawing or Conventional Ornament.
4. FREEHAND (PENCIL).	Stage I. and upwards.	Object and Model and Nature Drawing. Conventional Ornament and Design (the latter in combination with Mechanical Drawing).
5. OBJECT AND MODEL DRAWING.	Infants and Stage I.	Simple curved and straight-lined objects in the flat or round (the latter in simple elevation), including simple geometrical forms.
	Stages II. and III.	The same—more difficult profiles.

SUBJECT.	STAGE.	APPLICATION.—NATURE OF EXERCISES, ETC.
5. OBJECT AND MODEL DRAWING— *Continued.*	Stage IV.	Easy cylindrical and conical objects in upright positions.
	Stage V.	The same, including horizontal positions. Simple rectilineal objects in easy positions. Horizontal rectangular planes, *e.g.* drawing board.
	Stage VI.	The same with triangular and pyramidal objects. Simple groups of models and objects. Objects with simple attachments, *e.g.* handles, spouts, in easy elevation.
	Stage VII.	The same. More difficult positions. Inclined models and objects. Objects more irregular in form. More advanced groups.
	Stage IV. and upwards.	Models and objects to be drawn at varying levels (below or *above* the eye).
	Throughout the School.	Tone, colour, light and shade expressed simply in various media.
6. NATURE DRAWING.	Infants.	Simple leaves—pressed or otherwise in various media, in outline and mass. Simple venation. Simple flowers, fruits and vegetables. Picture-making with trees, grass, mountains, sea, sun, moon, etc.

SUBJECT.	STAGE.	APPLICATION.—NATURE OF EXERCISES, ETC.
6. NATURE DRAWING—*Continued.*	Stages I. and II.	*Simple natural objects without perspective.* Leaves without serrations. Leaves with few serrations. Easy buds and flowers. Common fruits and vegetables. Berries, seeds and nuts.
	Stages III. and IV.	*More difficult natural objects, including the study of serrations and junctions of stalks, but without perspective.* Flowers, leaves, fruits. Seeds and berries in groups. Simple sprays of leaves. Twigs and boughs of trees.
	Stages V. and VI.	*More advanced studies, including perspective and simple composition.* Flowers and buds. Sprays of leaves and flowers, including foreshortening. Ferns and seaweed. Ribbon-like leaves. Shells, feathers. Outdoor sketching of trees, clouds, etc.
7. COLOUR WORK. (*a*) *Crayon and Chalk.*	Infants and Stage I.	Mainly mass drawing applied to Object and Nature drawing on brown, tinted or white paper.
	Stage II. and upwards.	Expression of forms in "the round" on brown or tinted paper.
(*b*) *Direct Brushwork.*	Infants and Stage I.	Brush practice, straight and curved strokes. Simple leaf and flower forms. Outline drawing with the brush.

Subject.	Stage.	Application.—Nature of Exercises, etc.
(b) *Direct Brushwork—* (*Continued*).	Stage II.	More difficult brush strokes. Leaf forms, omitting serrations. Berries. Easy flower sprays.
	Stage III.	Mixing and matching colours. Brush strokes as before. Leaf and petal forms. Simple sprays.
	Stages IV., V., and VI.	Painting natural objects without outline :—see Nature Drawing Syllabus. Study of Colour.
(c) *Flat-tinting or washing.*	Stage III. and upwards.	Applied to Freehand Drawing of Conventional ornament, Nature and Object Drawing. Mapping, Mechanical Drawing (plans, elevations, etc.). Making of colour charts.
(d) *Painting.*	Stage IV. and upwards.	Exercises in tone values. Exercises in matching colours. Natural and artificial objects drawn in pencil and coloured with special regard to gradation of tone and colour.
8. CONVENTIONAL ORNAMENT AND DESIGN.	Stage I.	*Easy Ornamental Forms.* Simple leaf forms. Window tracing. Plain lettering.
	Stage II.	*Ornament derived from leaf and petal forms.* Study of leaves and petals. Bent iron-work patterns. Ornamental lettering. Rosettes.

SUBJECT.	STAGE.	APPLICATION.—NATURE OF EXERCISES, ETC.
8. C O N V E N-TIONAL ORNA-MENT AND DESIGN—*Continued.*	Stage III.	*More difficult ornaments derived from leaf and flower forms.* Exercises in design. The Anthemion. Lettering. Miscellaneous ornament.
	Stage IV.	*Simple classical ornament.* The Spiral in Nature and in Art. The Acanthus leaf. Grotesque ornament. Miscellaneous ornament. Exercises in Design.
	Stages V. and VI.	*Drawing from Photographs of Ornament,* and from specimens of wood-carving, textiles, pottery, etc. Design Exercises.
9. DRAWING IN LIGHT AND SHADE.	Stages. I.-III.	Pencil, crayon, or charcoal shading applied to drawing of objects by children at pleasure according to feeling.
	Stages IV. and V.	Definite methods applied to simple shading. Main principles illustrated.
	Stages VI. and VII.	More advanced shading of objects and casts by means of pencil, crayon, or brush.
10. Pen and Ink Work.	Stage IV. and upwards.	Objects and ornament in outline and with light and shade.
11. Memory Drawing.	Throughout the School.	
12. D r a w i n g from Imagination.	Throughout the School—mainly for Infants.	

EXAMINATION PAPERS

SET BY THE

BOARD OF EDUCATION

IN THE ELEMENTARY TEACHERS' CERTIFICATE
EXAMINATIONS.

December 1907.

*You may answer as many questions as you can ; but every candidate
is expected to attempt Questions 1 and 2.*

1. Suppose the diagram* to be the subject of a lesson in drawing
in outline. Show by means of a series of sketches the steps which
should be taken in making the drawing.

Make a drawing, such as might be used for the illustration of this
lesson, to show (*a*) how far the ornamental form in the diagram has
been inspired by a study and knowledge of Nature, or (*b*) how the
knowledge of some similar decorative form may have provided a
suggestion for the ornamental arrangement of the spray.

Draw also an object to which the decorative form in the diagram
might fitly be applied, and show the decoration in position.

Select what you consider to be one of the most beautiful features
of the diagram, and give your reasons, briefly and with explanatory
sketches, for thinking it beautiful.

2. A lesson on the drawing of a simple rectangular box in outline
is to be given to a class of twelve scholars seated at movable single
desks. Show by means of a sketch plan how you would arrange
the scholars, the box, and your blackboard.

Supposing the lesson to be of an hour's duration and the scholars
to be of varying attainments and ability, say how you would secure
that each individual should receive the amount of instruction
necessary to ensure due progress.

---

* A simple conventional spray of jessamine worked in embroidery.
The chief principle is " radiation."

Indicate by means of a series of sketches the steps which should be taken in making the drawing of the box.

Make a drawing, such as might add an element of vitality to such a lesson and enlarge the scholars' outlook, of some piece of furniture, architectural structure, or natural form, etc., in which some of the principles involved in drawing the box are exemplified.

3. State briefly how you would illustrate a lesson on one of the following subjects, making use of sketches in your statement :—

(a) a cow, cat, duck, or swallow ;

(b) the growth of a buttercup, daisy, crocus, honeysuckle, oak, holly, maple, or ash ;

(c) modes of transit.

4. Make a copy of the coloured pattern* with brush and colour. The parts of the pattern may be first indicated with the pencil.

5. A dimensioned sketch of a coffer is given.† Make a drawing of the coffer with instruments to the scale of $1\frac{1}{2}$ in. to 1 ft., and indicate clearly, by means of letters (A, B, etc.) or by written explanation, the steps taken in the construction of the drawing.

6. Describe in general terms a course of Drawing which you think suitable for a Public Elementary School including an Infants' Division.

December 1908.

Answer FOUR *questions,* ONE *only from each Section.*

SECTION I.

1. Explain briefly, with appropriate sketches, the following passage :—

> Here are sweet peas, on tiptoe for a flight,
> With wings of gentle flush o'er delicate white,
> And taper fingers catching at all things,
> To bind them all about with tiny rings.
>
> KEATS.

---

* Portion of embroidered border, consisting of two very simple spirals with conventional leaves.

† Elevation of a coffer with legs and lid. The actual dimensions are figured on the sketch.

2. Make a sketch to illustrate the following nursery rhyme :—

> Little Boy Blue, come blow up your horn,   ·
> The sheep's in the meadow, the cow's in the corn.
> Where's Little Boy Blue that looks after the sheep?
> He's under the haycock fast asleep.

3. Explain with sketches any five of the following words from Scott's " Ivanhoe " :—

Halberd, beaver, arched barbican, corselet, bartizan, casque, escutcheon, visor, barret cap.

Section II.

1. Sketch in water-colours, broadly treated, a group of three common objects which would be suitable for a drawing lesson to Standard VII.

Make a plan showing (*a*) the arrangement of the desks, (*b*) the number of children, and (*c*) the position of the group in relation to the children.

2. Indicate by sketches a short series of graded exercises in colour suitable for drawing lessons to a first class of infants.

What materials would you use, and what arrangements would you make for supplying them to the children so as to prevent loss of time ?

State the length and number of the lessons you have in mind for the series.

3. Make a series of drawings, one of which should be in colour, to illustrate a lesson on the development of—

> (*a*) a plant from the seed ; or
> (*b*) a butterfly from the egg.

State the class for which the lesson is intended.

Section III.

1. State briefly what are the chief dangers to be guarded against in teaching nature-drawing in elementary schools, and say how you would obviate these dangers.

Illustrate your answer by sketches.

2. A girls' school of seven standards in a town is about to take drawing for the first time. Draw up a course such as you would suggest under these circumstances.

What general explanation of aim and method would you give for the guidance of the class teachers ?

3. State the chief difficulties you have met with in teaching children to draw directly from objects, and explain with sketches the methods you have adopted in trying to overcome them.

Section IV.

1. Make a sketch for a carpenter's trestle and indicate upon it by dimension lines the measurements which you would expect scholars to make with a view to drawing to scale its side and end elevations.

Construct a plain scale of feet and inches, 2 inches to 1 foot, and, having chosen suitable dimensions for the trestle, draw the side and end elevations to that scale.

2. Construct a scale showing 10 feet to an inch, and use it to solve the following by geometrical construction and measurement.

Problem :—A ladder 30 feet in length will just reach the top of a wall when the foot of the ladder is distant 12 feet from that of the wall.

Find the height of the wall and the distance from its base at which the foot of a ladder 45 feet long must be placed so as just to reach the top.

December 1909.

Answer FOUR *questions,* ONE *only from each Section.*

Section I.

Make any drawings which you consider suitable to illustrate *one* of the following passages :—

1.   O velvet bee, you're a dusty fellow,
       You've powdered your legs with gold !
       O brave marsh marybuds, rich and yellow,
       Give me your money to hold.
                                     JEAN INGELOW.

2. "The pale moon, which had hitherto been contending with the flitting clouds, now shone out, and gave them a view of the solitary and naked tower, situated on a projecting cliff that beetled on the German Ocean."
                       SCOTT.—*The Bride of Lammermoor.*

3.   This is the Cat,
       That killed the Rat,
       That ate the Malt,
       That lay in the House that Jack built.
                                     (Nursery Rhyme.)

Section II.

1. How would you proceed in giving a first lesson in colour mixing to a class provided with three pigments, Prussian Blue, Crimson Lake, and Gamboge?

Illustrate your answer by a series of tints, and state the approximate age of the children for whom the lesson is intended.

2. Make a water-colour drawing, showing the treatment that might reasonably be expected from a scholar in the highest class of a senior department, of one of the following flowers :—pansy, tulip, wall-flower, periwinkle, dog-rose.

3. Make a sketch in water-colours showing a pleasing arrangement of three or four simple common objects with which you are familiar.
State the age of the children for whom the group would be suitable.

SECTION III.

1. Sketch a common object suitable for a drawing lesson to Standard III., and state your reasons for the selection.
What object would you have used in the preceding drawing lesson, and what object would you propose for the next drawing lesson?

2. Show by a series of sketches how the drawing of a common object such as a cup, saucer, etc., may be directly helpful in drawing certain natural objects.

3. Make three drawings to illustrate the kind of object suitable for a first class of infants to draw—

    (a) on the blackboard with chalk,

    (b) on brown or grey paper with coloured crayons,

    (c) on white paper with brush and water-colour.

Give your reasons for thinking the object suitable.

SECTION IV.

1. Sketch from memory a common wooden soap-box made to hang on a wall.
Mark it with suitable dimensions, and draw as near to full scale as your paper will allow the development-plan necessary for the construction of a complete paper model, ignoring the thickness of the wood.

2. Make a dimensioned sketch of a common kitchen table with one drawer.
Construct a scale of one and a half inches to a foot, and draw with instruments the front and side elevations of the table.

INDEX.